Freelance Writing for Newspapers

Books in the 'Writing Handbooks' series

Developing Characters for Script Writing • Rib Davis
Freelance Copywriting • Diana Wimbs
Marketing your Book: An Author's Guide • Alison Baverstock
Writing for Children • Margaret Clark
Writing Comedy • John Byrne
Writing Crime Fiction • H.R.F. Keating
Writing Dialogue for Scripts • Rib Davis
Writing Erotic Fiction • Derek Parker
Writing Fantasy and Science Fiction • Lisa Tuttle
Writing Horror Fiction • Guy N. Smith
Writing for a Living • Michael Legat
Writing for Magazines • Jill Dick
Writing a Play • Steve Gooch
Writing Poetry • John Whitworth
Writing Popular Fiction • Rona Randall
Writing for Radio • Rosemary Horstmann
Writing Romantic Fiction • Daphne Clair and Robyn Donald
Writing for Soaps • Chris Curry
Writing Successful Textbooks • Anthony Haynes
Writing for Television • Gerald Kelsey
Writing a Thriller • André Jute
Writing about Travel • Morag Campbell

Other books for writers

Creative Web Writing • Jane Dorner
The Internet: A Writer's Guide • Jane Dorner
Novel Writing • Evan Marshall
The Reader's Encyclopedia • William Rose Benét
Research for Writers • Ann Hoffmann
Rewriting: a creative approach to writing fiction • David Michael Kaplan
Word Power: a guide to creative writing • Julian Birkett
Writers' and Artists' Yearbook

Writing Handbooks

Freelance Writing for Newspapers

THIRD EDITION

Jill Dick

A & C Black • London

To Jim

Third edition 2003
Second edition 1998
First published 1991

A & C Black Publishers Limited
37 Soho Square, London W1D 3QZ
www.acblack.com

ISBN 0–7136–6363–4

A CIP catalogue record for this book is
available from the British Library.

A & C Black uses paper produced with elemental
chlorine-free pulp, harvested from managed
sustainable forests.

Typeset in 10½ on 12½ pt Sabon
Printed and bound in Great Britain by
Creative Print and Design (Wales), Ebbw Vale

Contents

Standfirst

In newspaper terms, a 'standfirst' does just that. It stands first and alone, to tempt readers into reading the piece to which it refers on a later page. Although it cannot stand alone in a book, this standfirst fulfils its other purpose: to give readers a foretaste of what's in store.

In these pages you will find techniques and working tips that journalists pick up over a lifetime in the job. Discover who does what – and how – in the making of a newspaper, where freelances fit into the editor's plans and the importance of advertising.

Read about the huge range of markets available for freelance copy – in local, free, national and provincial papers. Learn how to identify readership, who owns which papers and how to approach editors.

What to write? You'll never run short of ideas again. Using specialist knowledge, reviewing, writing small pieces to please editors: it's all here. Find out what style *is* and how to build your copy; importantly, too, how to *re*write, using 'insider' tricks of the trade.

Appreciate the skills needed for successful interviewing and the value of research, learn how to use technology to your advantage and to deal (as simply and effectively as possible) with the business side of being a freelance writer, and find out about self-assessment of income tax, keeping records, training, copyright, rates of pay, being paid – and more.

As freelances – and of course, 'he' is equally 'she' throughout this book – the whole gamut of writing activities is open to us. We can be reporters, dealing largely or exclusively with news, feature writers delving into and developing individual stories at greater depth, reviewers of books, films or theatre, or specialist writers on a wide assortment of topics. Whatever the finished product, it is the result of craftsmanship unobserved by readers.

Here you will learn, as thousands of people who write for newspapers have learned, that it is always the ordinary people behind a story that make it live. Without people there would be no news, for to a journalist they are the breath of life. It is also important to understand and recognise our own feelings if we are to express them in words for readers; unless we can do so we won't be able to recognise them in other people.

One thing this book can't do is teach you to write – no book can do that. It is only by sitting down and *writing* that anyone becomes a writer. But here you will see yourself and your work as an essential part of the newspaper business – and that is the first step to success.

1. What is a Freelance?

'It must be true. It was in the paper.'

We used to hear that said. Nowadays, alas, we have learned to be more suspicious about newspapers and what they publish. Journalists are low in the public's esteem – even lower than politicians (and that's saying something). This is as sad for the great newspaper-reading public as it is for journalists trained to uphold the integrity of the press – and the great majority who do so. We know that newspapers sometimes fall short of the highest standards, but we also understand that the market is fiercely competitive; the temptation to embroider, exaggerate and distort newspaper copy is considerable. Exciting and revealing stories about people in the public eye are always interesting, and papers founded with the intention of printing only good news have short lives. Too often we read of reporters harassing victims of crime or misfortune, while biased, ill-informed and factually distorted copy appears in print somewhere every day. The power of the press is not always used wisely.

For all their long traditions, newspapers are sobered by the cognisance that they are, and always will be, the servants rather than the masters of the people. Just let enough people stop buying a paper, however well-established or important, and its future wavers. What can we do – what can *you* do – to improve our reputation? Being in a position to write about other people imposes on us a moral responsibility to tell the truth as it appears to us. That means not only in news reports or when dealing with facts and figures, but also in the way in which we represent people, their circumstances and their lives. We must never belittle them or write anything to make them look foolish or less worthy than we find them. Just as speech may be given variety of meaning if accompanied by raised eyebrows or a mock-severity, so what we write may be carelessly (or deliberately) laden with innuendo: the journalistic sneer, the glib approach, the suave assertions made over innocent people's heads. Such insinuation cheapens journalism because it is writing with less than honesty. If we want the public to trust us we must first show ourselves to be trustworthy.

The death of Diana, Princess of Wales, caused a decline in the sales of nationals, especially the tabloids. After the funeral and repeated speculation about the circumstances of her death, papers realised that their major front-page star – always a good seller – had gone. Circulation was always boosted by a good picture of Diana on the front page, and there was a limit to how long the tabloids could extend the talk surrounding her death. Newspapers are also aware that such is the advance of technology (no longer 'new') and the speed of information delivery that long gone are the days when they were the first messengers to break news to the general or local public.

Fleet Street and the surrounding areas were the traditional home of British newspapers: the *Financial Times* was near St Paul's, *The Times* at Blackfriars, the *Sunday Times* and *Sunday Pictorial* in Gray's Inn Road. The old 'home' is virtually deserted by them now and the phrase 'Fleet Street' exists to refer to a broad swathe of national newspapers rather than to their geographical location. When in 1986 Rupert Murdoch made the first move out to Canary Wharf, one of the highest buildings in the world, in the rebuilt dock area of east London, he wrote a landmark in the British press of far greater significance than merely moving offices. He had broken the stranglehold of the print unions, changed the working life of every journalist, freelance or otherwise. Yes, you too, if you want to write for newspapers.

Newspapers aren't just about news – they're about lifestyle, travel, cooking, home, fashion and a host of other topics that are in constant need of freelance contributions. People in the news may be rich or famous, or they may be just ordinary folk who make good 'copy' for a wide variety of reasons. It's good because, well-written, it allows readers to live and learn through others, and perhaps to understand a little bit more about the world we live in and what makes us all tick.

Look at any newspaper and note how many 'stories' fill the pages. (Of course to a journalist, the word 'story' has nothing to do with fiction; it just means a piece of writing, be it a report, a news item, a feature, or anything else – and any story is what we call 'copy'.) News, travel, entertainment, sport, food, the arts, local and national events, business – the range of topics covered in any single edition can be very wide. The dailies will put a completely different and new issue out tomorrow, or even again *today* in a later edition, and the weeklies cover all this – and often more – once a week. Specialist papers run to many pages, and weekend supplements issued with major Saturday and Sunday newspapers run to a great many. All this means that a lot of people behind the scenes are writing copy that is good enough and topical enough to fill countless acres of newsprint. The leading papers subscribe to agency services for some stories, and their own staff write others. But virtually all papers everywhere look to freelances *of the right calibre* to provide copy with individual, fresh and innovative appeal.

Study the markets, do your research, write well and sell your work to newspapers: that's what being a freelance is all about. You're not on a staff contract and are solely responsible for finding ideas, writing, selling your work, getting paid, and every other aspect of the job. You may find yourself up against trained journalists, many of them highly specialised and experienced with books full of useful contacts made over the years. To cut costs, more papers now employ them as freelances rather than as staff writers, so nobody should kid you that your path will be easy. Worthwhile? A thousand times YES. Just a matter of knocking off a few pieces now and then when you feel like it, without much effort? NO. But turn yourself into just what an editor wants: a writer who can supply what is needed, at the right time and to the right length, who will not object when asked to make changes, who will not be a nuisance by ringing with trivial questions that should have been settled at the beginning, and who will always remember that the editor's decision is final; do this and you're in – welcomed with open arms.

Writing for newspapers and selling to them means entering the hard and sometimes cold world of business, and occasionally you may feel that everyone is against you. But first impressions are misleading; persevere and you'll find your feet.

Above all, enjoy writing – there's not much point in doing it if you don't.

Getting to work

Be practical. Start with local or trade papers where competition is lighter and you can find your own way. Build a portfolio to demonstrate your writing ability to the next editor you approach, moving up a step at a time. Every piece you write will smooth your path.

Read and write something every day. There is no better way to improve your writing. Read newspapers as a writer, assessing what you are reading and what the writer is saying. Think about why the piece is written as it is, who the readers are and what they will make of it. Read about the newspaper industry, what makes it live and how you can be part of it. Join writing clubs, search the internet for writers' resources, buy writers' market books, get insider newsletters. Talk to successful writers who've written what you want to write and who can show you the way – and keep writing. Every successful writer in the world (not only in the newspaper industry) started as a raw beginner, knowing nothing. Each one climbed the ladder – and so can you. Practise, practise, practise.

Some freelances never do better than work hard with no pension, no sick pay, no expense accounts, free stationery or perks, no paid holidays and no contractual continuity or security. Others are now top names in the world of newspapers; you might assume many of them to be staff employees, so regularly or frequently is their copy published. They *choose* freelance status: they relish the freedom to work when and where they like, organising and running their own working lives as they want to. Freelances don't work in newspaper offices and are not on the payroll of any paper; they just take it upon themselves to submit what they write to editors, hoping that they will like it enough to print it and pay for it.

Anyone can be a freelance, but dedication to the task is vital. You may get a few ideas today, research into them a little next week and write your piece a month later, and even that unhurried approach will require a degree of discipline if your work is to be publishable. Tighten up the schedule, determining that by a particular date or within a pre-arranged time you will think, study, research, write, rewrite and rewrite again – however many times it takes before you are satisfied – and a firm plan of action becomes necessary. There is no 'right' way and no 'wrong' way. Only the quality and timing of what you write will determine how successful you will be.

Even firmly established freelances at the top of the tree know they will only stay there if their work continues to be the best. Of course they've experienced rejections – and they don't forget them. Yet failure always was the mother of success, and success is a journey rather than a destination. Meeting the challenge of continual disappointment with a strong determination to succeed will certainly prove any writer's ability; that's the professional way. And it's amazing that the more professional you are, the more editors need you.

Be a freelance journalist and you shoulder a responsibility that will keep you on your toes. If you are fascinated by people, what they do and think, why, where, how and when, you'll find it challenging and exhilarating, demanding and satisfying: immensely rewarding in every way. When the ink gets into your veins, there's no job to beat it.

2. Who Does What?

At the 'sharp' end of its life, your local newspaper may be run, by just a handful of hard-working men and women. But almost all local weeklies are owned by one or another of some 20 large publishers, so every small-town local paper is probably a small cog (or perhaps not so small, in a heavily populated area) in a big publishing machine. Despite this you can be sure that every paper, high or low, rich or poor, is unique. What makes it so is the editor and the team that he can gather round him. If the team numbers just a few, most of them will be able to turn their hands to a variety of tasks. Despite such versatility (or perhaps because of it) everyone in the team knows, and adheres to, a clearly and carefully defined working pattern. An awareness of deadlines rules the day – and often the night as well.

At all levels – national, regional and local – the production of a newspaper is generally organised into five distinct departments. Readers of this book will be mostly concerned about the *editorial* department, but an awareness of the work of other departments is invaluable in gaining an overall sense of where and how we freelances fit into the picture. Of the other main departments, *administration* deals with the building, secretarial, financial and stationery matters (just as in any business). The *production* side copes with paper, machinery and the composing and printing of the paper. Finally there are *sales* (including distribution), and *advertising*. Of the five departments only advertising and sales generate income. Even the sales department sometimes runs at a net loss, having enormous expenses in itself. What a weight of responsibility rests on advertising!

Newspaper pages are made up of advertisements, headlines, body text and pictures (commonly known as 'pix'). You may think that I have those in the wrong order of importance, headlines and pictures being more important than advertising; but in today's tough world, publishing newspapers is not just about writing – it's a business. For a newspaper to remain viable, advertising takes priority. Advertisements, not news, are allotted their places first when the process of turning blank sheets of newsprint into a finished newspaper begins. Well before publication discussions between advertising agents and the paper's representatives will have determined the size, shape and design of the display and classified advertisements. The overall plan for each edition is carefully balanced and often precise pages and positions on them have been negotiated and paid for by advertisers. For every edition the advertising department produces what is known as a 'dummy', showing all the pages and which spaces on each have been sold to particular advertisers. It is these dummies that provide a basic framework on which the editor and his team set to work when the planning and progress of the day's edition is checked.

Not all the journalists on the payroll of leading national dailies are likely to be writers; there are many other jobs to be done. On regional papers even fewer of the total number of employees spend their time writing. For instance, with pages of advertisements and restricted editorial space, a small weekly may have only a handful of people writing to fill it. So we writers aren't the most important people? I'm afraid not. Heading the importance league are the teams involved in distribution – and they work very hard indeed. Their job is to get the papers (in the right quantity and at the right time, too, which is vital) to places where the public can and will buy them. If the finished paper is not available on sale, all the effort and dedication of everyone else working on it, including the writers, will be wasted. Nor do we come second in the pecking order. That goes to the page designers – particularly the front-page designers. The paper may be on sale when and where people expect to find it, but a lot of buying is done on impulse. If the front page is not instantly pleasing to the eye then the paper will not be bought in sufficient numbers to render the whole enterprise viable.

Only then, in third position of importance, come the writers. Yes, now we come into our own for what we write makes or breaks the paper. The editor knows this, everyone else on his staff knows this – and freelances know it too. We, as much as any staff writers, can take comfort from being as essential a part in the highly structured organisational plan as are many other employees in the making of a newspaper. And if you ever find yourself thinking that being a freelance is a job too hard, remember that it is also hard to become an airline pilot, a doctor or a champion tennis-player. One of the comments from editors that I don't like hearing, but have to accept, is that too many would-be freelances don't try hard enough.

When the BBC and the *Guardian* ran a writers' competition a few years ago, entries flooded in from freelances. Presenter and judge John Diamond had to report that the overall standard of submissions was very low. An amateurish approach, simple mistakes and a failure to understand what was required for the job characterised most of the entries. The one consolation to be drawn from this depressing situation is that with so many freelances turning in sub-standard work, it should leave the way clear for those determined to do better – a great deal better. Nothing worthwhile was ever achieved without hard work.

The editor

The editor of a national newspaper is like the manager of any business. He is the overseer of all departments, responsible for the whole content as well as for the style and image of the paper – and answerable to his superiors who may be constantly breathing down his neck. He may work at the daily or weekly job himself if he is not busy with administrative matters, meetings etc. or he may play a more supervisory role. Some editors have risen from a background of reporting or feature-writing and enjoy still being part of the writing team, composing their own leader columns and being involved with the running of all departments; others leave the staff to run the day-to-day business. On smaller papers where staff numbers are lower, the editor won't be able to sit in policy-making solitude for long and may spend days as busily as any of the staff, turning to any job in the office that needs doing. It's a man-of-all-work editor for the small papers, an editor-in-chief with deputies and assistants for the big ones and usually a mixture of both between the two.

If the editor is ill or on holiday the deputy or assistant editors take over, if any are appointed, for they rank in seniority between the editor and the heads of various departments or sections of the paper. How many of these exist will depend on the size, circulation and publication frequency of individual titles. On the editor's shoulders rests the ultimate responsibility. If there are complaints against the paper he must deal with them, and if it's late coming out he has to accept the blame – regardless of what caused it to be delayed and who else might have been more directly responsible. Speed is everything for a newspaper's life is short – at the most a fortnight, sometimes a week, perhaps only a day and often just a few hours. Failing to meet production deadlines is dire; the penalty for delay will be a day's work lost, and possibly even the editor's head.

In the day-to-day working pattern the editor works with his team to decide how to fill the space allotted for each edition with text, headlines and pictures. There will have been a lot of pre-planning and this is where the editor will have been spending some of his time. Sales folk will have sold space for display and classified advertisements and the spaces for them will already have been allocated, as they always go in first.

Weekly papers do not have to work at such a pace, but on a daily paper, specialist columns will already be set up or on the planning menu from decisions made the day before or even two days earlier. There will be similar matters to settle for editions for tomorrow or for several days ahead as well as urgent decisions to be made about the next immediate edition. Just as customers revisit the same supermarket because they know where to find the goods they want, readers are happier with a familiar layout – so making the paper attractive while keeping it as regular readers like it is another task falling to the editor. Balancing this with the need for a bright, attractive appearance is not easy.

Careful attention is given to the appearance of regular parts of the paper. Tabloids are usually seven columns wide and broadsheets generally eight or nine. Various sections of the paper are instantly recognisable by their distinctive typefaces and layout formats. So a headline for a gripping news item will use a different typeface from one over a piece quoting stock-market prices, and lists such as radio or television programmes are given individual and easily read typefaces. That's the way readers like it – a matter always in the forefront of the editor's mind.

Space for features is governed by the paper's size, as well as the amount of space absorbed by advertisements and news. The former bring in revenue; the latter, with rare exceptions, has to be paid for. Features also cost money (though not enough, in the opinion of many freelance recipients of it) but they are exclusive and valuable to the paper. A leader writer will have had talks with the editor (if he is not writing it himself) and decisions will have been made about the topic of the lead, its width and length. Regular pieces like TV pages (if not in a separate section which will be dealt with by its own team), the weather forecast and the crossword puzzle, for instance, will have been slotted in place and the only spaces left will be reserved for the 'hard' news that may come in before production time.

Editors have to juggle many balls in the air at the same time. Local and smaller papers serving a defined circulation area get their up-to-date news of what's happening by doing the 'calls' – just asking around. Other news stories will originate from readers phoning in with tip-offs about interesting items that might be worth following up. Press releases about forthcoming events will already be in the pipeline while new matters pour into major newspaper offices all the time. Some will carry the germ of a newsworthy story sufficiently interesting for a reporter to investigate. For the big papers the most valuable providers of news are the agencies set up all over the world to gather news from the globe. American scientists list 'setting up a news agency' as high in their priorities when settling men on Mars. Modern technology has had a profound effect on the methods of distributing news; some 20 million words per day are received by various newspapers in London 'on the wire'.

The editor decides – or his team decides with his approval – where features and news will sit on the pages or sections of pages allotted to them. If your accepted feature gets a 'good' place on the page (that's traditionally a little right of centre on the top half of a right-hand page – a spot to which, experts tell us, the eye is most naturally drawn) you can be reasonably confident that it was considered important enough to hold that place. This doesn't mean, of course, that other spots in the paper are not important. Computer typesetting makes it easy to move whole stories from one place to another on the page-layout screen and pages are designed to please the eye – of both editor and reader. The practice developed a long time ago that a story anywhere on the front page 'above the line' (i.e. above the half-way fold, where the bottom half of the paper might not be visible in a newsagent's rack or on his counter) presented such a great sales factor that it should attract a higher rate of pay than the same story would in a less valued position. The truth is that every story in the paper is valuable for that day's issue or it wouldn't be there. Everything in this cut-throat world of competition is cosseted most carefully and each story, each picture, each word must earn its place.

Much of the news that comes in all the time will not make readers gasp, for it is already expected. It could be the result of a big football match or a report of a major race meeting, the verdict in a keenly followed trial, a statement from a hospital following a serious fire in a hotel in which several people were injured, or just the latest weather forecast. Such 'news' cannot be to hand at the early planning stage. One way and another through avenues well-established and just occasionally by unexpected routes the news comes in and eventually (if considered worthy) takes its place in the day's layout.

The editor's team – including freelances

Most national and regional morning papers go to press in the small hours of the morning and the hours leading up to that time are every bit as busy, albeit in a different way, as those of daylight. The night editor heads his own team and is almost as important as the editor.

When most freelance writers think of writing for newspapers they automatically think of features and more freelance feature material comes into the average newspaper than any other sort of freelance copy. All editorial content, i.e. non-advertising, is either news or features, so high-circulation papers employ both a news editor and a features editor. We will be in most contact with the latter whose duties include briefing freelances, discussing their work, checking copy and seeing that payment matters are passed on to the accounts department. Newspapers are always up to date: time and season are inescapable concepts to bear in mind for all feature copy must be hung on 'pegs' of current news. Sections of a paper involving the features editor might include Letters-to-the-Editor, horoscopes, in-depth investigative features, holidays, the diary column, cookery, fashion, health, gardening, children's interests, the home, showbiz, crosswords, interviews and the gossip column. He might also have to deal with other topics such as motoring that (on some papers) may be the province of specialist writers.

The larger a newspaper the more it can afford to pay specialists to write on individual topics. These writers will often be freelances who have gained a 'standby' place among the paper's contacts by having previously impressed the editor or features editor with their expertise and ability. Specialists generally cover topics like music and have proven track records. Study of your own paper will reveal regularly published columns or show that the same columnist is on hand with an authoritative view on, say, railway matters at the time of any major rail crash. Wise beginners will avoid these topics and spot ones that do not feature regularly.

A feature by a well-known writer carries facts and figures often brought in to support a particular line of thought or a special point. However, its main purpose is to explain, elucidate and expand before reaching a conclusion, generally based on a particular aspect of the news. Such feature writers give papers flavour and originality and many papers are sold because readers respect their opinions. Their words give copy rhythm and colour in the most appropriate style for the market. Top feature writers will be highly rewarded.

Such is the pressure of work on a big daily that there will be city, political, foreign and sports editors. Where there is a separate section devoted to a specific topic, within the features editor's aegis, it will probably have its own editor (and maybe even assistants) as well as staff writers and reporters attached for varying periods. Leading papers will also employ regular and occasional overseas correspondents, almost certainly based in key cities round the world, who will always be prepared to fly to 'flash points' within their reach when required.

Political and parliamentary correspondents are highly skilled and experienced writers who are rarely seen. They spend most of their time at Westminster and such work is not likely to be the province of beginner freelances – although holders of these posts with sufficient training and experience behind them may prefer to work as freelances. Their job is to report on parliamentary debates and affairs and to write notes and sketches. Lobby correspondents are busy sounding out what's going on behind the scenes, writing background reports and trying to interpret government actions and ideas. They receive information provided by government spokespeople but you'll seldom get them to admit what's going on for it's usually off the record.

The news editor looks after all incoming news, while the foreign editor (if there is one) is responsible for selecting and working on the copy of foreign correspondents and on stories coming in from overseas. All the news – from whatever source, on whatever topic and whenever it arrives – is balanced with features, perhaps already placed, and rearrangement of copy is commonplace.

Reporters

Reporters can be any age, and even if you're not intending to be one for very long, a spell as a reporter or village correspondent on a local newspaper works wonders for self-confidence in the world of journalism. Reporters are the hard-working men and women at the very root of a newspaper. They are likely to be out and about collecting information from tip-offs supplied by the office, waiting to file the latest news on a 'running' story or carrying out any one of a dozen duties in the circulation area. Reporting may be considered to be the bottom rung of the ladder in the newspaper world but it's the place where many a leading journalist began learning the craft. A reporter or a local correspondent carries considerable responsibility: he may be fresh out of training school or an older, more experienced writer who doesn't want to change jobs; on papers covering a wide geographical area he's probably overworked as well.

Unless somebody tells them what is going on, especially in country districts, weeklies cannot hope to find out what is happening in every town and village and many events will go unreported, to the dissatisfaction of readers. Being a reporter is a challenging job and one that should not be undertaken without careful consideration. Maintaining a flow of news can be a chore when you want to go on holiday or if you are ill. Weekly reporters may receive only a small remuneration – but the first rule of the job is never to let the community down.

Doing the 'calls' is a regular task. This means calling on the people or organisations likely to provide news: the police and fire stations, local hospitals, the Town Hall, the Citizens Advice Bureau, the morgue, the courts, schools, clubs, health clinics, leisure and community centres – anywhere and everywhere in the locality where someone in authority is able and willing to impart news or the basis of a news story to investigate and pass on to readers of the paper. Once contacts are established they can be encouraged to make contact with the paper themselves when they have anything to report.

As a welcome by-product, reporting skills benefit out of all proportion to the apparently humdrum level of the reporter's job. Making quick decisions about copy, learning how to present it clearly in print, by email and over the phone, developing an increasing awareness about what is and what is not newsworthy, and enjoying a growing ease in the job – all this makes being a reporter a very worthwhile task for a freelance at any stage. It is also very satisfying. For countless readers the local reporter is the only 'real' journalist they see or ever will see, so their opinion of the newspaper will depend on him. Illogical and slightly daunting this may be but it is an extra reason for a freelance to do the job well and enjoy doing it.

Court reporting and proceedings

Freelance writers are not often called on to report court proceedings and it is easy to understand why this is so. But learning how to do this fascinating job adds more power to your arm when offering your services to a newspaper editor.

A thorough familiarity with the procedure in various types of court, a well-filled 'contacts' book, a fluent shorthand note and a basic knowledge of the law are minimum requirements. In theory a reporting journalist is supposed to be the representative of the general public, telling them what happened to whom and how the proceedings were conducted. There are not enough court reporters on the staff of newspapers to cover anything like all the courts sitting at any one time so you might think freelances would be welcomed – but even those with experience in other fields may not be good court reporters.

Sensitivity to the nature of a job involving serious decisions affecting people's lives and futures, unlimited discretion and loyalty, reserves of patience, an understanding of libel and contempt and – above all – the ability to report facts, figures and speeches with as much honest impartiality as anyone can muster; do you fit the bill? When you come to writing your reports you must learn not to use legal jargon in a situation where you will have heard plenty. Your readers won't understand it; they want to know what the case is all about, who is involved and how it ended. Names, facts, dates, times, sentences – these are what makes readers sit up. (They can also make headlines or be the stuff of stories for future editions of your paper, after the court reporting has finished.)

Many laws exist which prevent disclosure of certain information in certain circumstances and if you are not aware of them it is possible to break them. As in all such matters, ignorance of the law is no defence. Even if you are never likely to find yourself in this position, knowing where to find official help could be invaluable. All types of courts have their own traditions and practices, but common to all is the sight of someone who has fallen foul of the law being subjected to its jurisdiction. Be a court reporter and you'll find that all human life is indeed there. It will teach you a great deal about the law and even more about humanity.

Sub-editors

Subs, as sub-editors may be called, have the job of ensuring that all staff-written and freelance copy is ready to be printed. The chief subs and their teams exert a great impact on how the paper will look when it is finished. Their tasks include checking facts, correcting grammar and punctuation to conform to the house style, writing crossheads and headlines with setting instructions (headlines sell papers, especially on Sundays), and inserting instructions about the size, shape and typography of each story.

After editorial conferences during the course of an edition's preparation, the pre-print business of the day is not complete until the subs have finished their work. They are often not popular with writers. 'They only want to ruin our copy,' is a common complaint, and there is no doubt that sometimes what appears in print doesn't sit happily with what the writer wanted to or hoped would appear. But much of the misunderstanding is due to ignorance: not only (although sometimes) on the part of the subs, but also on the part of the writers. Few freelances have the chance to see subs at work and to understand the difficulties they face. Phrases like 'repeat himself again and again', 'come to a complete halt' and 'every single day' do not, as some writers imagine, make a sub jump for gleeful joy and reach for the proverbial blue pencil; more probably he sighs and wonders if writers will ever learn. As someone who has been a staff writer, a sub-editor and a freelance journalist, I can see faults on all sides.

Typography is a fascinating subject, and the ability to select the right typeface and use it to best effect is a most valuable skill. Type is measured in points, a point being 0.01383 of an inch, which gives approximately 72 points to the inch. This refers to the depth of the body of metal on which a letter stands, not to the actual size of the letter. Because there are small bevels at the top and bottom of the little metal block, the actual face size is always less than the body size. To establish a working norm it is accepted in the printing world that the point size equals the total size of the lower-case alphabet. This is measured from the top of the highest 'ascender' (d, for instance) to the bottom of the lowest 'descender' (like q).

Consider how you would interpret a sub-editor's job specification: to shape the material in the form of presentation decided by the chief sub so as to bring out the point of a story, to condense it more effectively than can be done by cutting and to make it more readable. To have a sound knowledge of the laws of libel and contempt, of central and local government organisation, of the various types of court and the pitfalls to be avoided when reporting from them, of newspaper terms, of the organisation for which he works and of the paper's edition times, with deadlines for copy, pix and pages. And there's more: to be ready to deal with copy arriving often in quantity and certainly with increasing speed and urgency as the paper's deadline approaches. And even more – to ensure that copy is in good taste and good English while observing the writer's own concept and the needs of the reader.

On top of all this, subs also cope with copy from reporters, news agencies, public relations and publicity sources. They prepare the text with all the acknowledged methods of marking, advise layout subs on story length and page layout, maybe write revised stories to include later material on those already running, handle pictures, probably act as copy-tasters, selecting stories for special importance, human interest and entertainment value. Through all of this they must keep calm and practical. Quite an exacting job, isn't it? As a great deal of a paper's success depends on how it looks – sales being in known relation to appearance, rather than to news content – the best tabloid headline and layout subs are deservedly well paid.

On national papers, the front page is generally the last to be 'put to bed' in order to maintain topicality until the very last moment. Then, when the editor is satisfied that everything is in order, it's time for the many skilled people who have been handling the current edition to hand it over.

Putting it away

The change in newspaper production methods has been so rapid that it has been likened to a second industrial revolution – even greater that of 1477, when William Caxton printed *Dictes and Sayenges of the Phylosophers*, the first dated book produced in England. As I write, even more advances are on the way – but not everyone gives such changes an undiluted welcome. Perhaps change can never shake off its shadow of problems.

Older journalists recall the excitement of the first days of the 'new' technology, which seemed little short of a miracle of design and ingenuity. Photo-typesetting replaced 'hot' metal and the (literally) revolutionary rotary press saw the beginning of the end of the old hand-set flatbed printing. Rotary printing involves plates of text set into cylinders and enormous rolls of newsprint. The inked plates are forced onto the paper which is printed on both sides at incredible speed before being cut, folded and stacked to the required finish. (The first time I saw the presses thundering out the *News of the World* was like watching one of the wonders of the modern world – and the intoxicating smell of it has never left me.)

Then came computerised layout and design in the office environment, which allows the easy make-up of pages of text and pix on screen. Most copy is not written on paper in the office but by direct input on the keyboard. With the copy on screen in front of them, journalists can delete errors, insert sentences, move whole paragraphs and blocks or import them from elsewhere, all at the touch of a key, in a sophisticated version of what we can all now do on our home computers. Completed pages are then photographed and set in the negative to be fused onto polymer sheets for web-offset litho or letterpress printing. It is called off-set litho printing because there is no direct printing from the plate onto the paper. If there were, the image on the plate would quickly be destroyed. Nor does the miracle end there. If, for instance, the editorial and advertising preparation is to be done in one place and the actual printing is to be done elsewhere, perhaps in several widely separated print units in other parts of the UK or even of the world – another marvel takes over. By 'facsimile transmission' it takes no longer and is equally easy to print the paper in a different country. There is much to marvel at in today's newspaper production and the experts tell us there is plenty more ahead.

Advertisers

Advertisements are always positioned before anything else and there are several reasons why this is so. The first is that advertisers are paying the paper, i.e. buying the space their advertisements occupy. Although many newspaper proprietors would have you believe that their pages hold advertisements for more altruistic reasons, there is no doubt that the money received from advertisers – especially the big, regular spenders – is the life-blood of newspapers. It is not unusual for a Sunday newspaper to reserve more than half of the paper for advertisements. The total income to newspapers is colossal: in 2000, national papers sold advertising space to the value of £2,257,000, while local papers did even better with a revenue of £2,763,000.

The true value of advertising is more extensive than may at first appear. The wider the paper's circulation and extent of its selling points, the more outlets there are for an advertiser's message. His bargaining power grows even though his feedback from readers is more difficult to record. Advertisers know, too, that they are even more easily blown about by the fortunes of the times than are newspapers themselves. The country's overall economic position will give an indication of the current health of the newspaper business; is a recession round the corner, are interest rates low, is unemployment rising? Matters way outside the newspaper world will affect all papers (yes, your local weekly as well), to a greater or lesser degree depending on how much they rely on selling their advertising space.

British newspapers are zero-rated for Value Added Tax but are not subsidised. If they didn't accept advertising their cover prices would be much higher, sales would be low and many would go out of business. Advertising revenue and sales are their only sources of income, and they are tender plants that need careful nurturing. As one example, the collapse of Communism in much of eastern Europe at the end of the 1980s dealt a severe blow to the *Morning Star*. When the Soviet Union cut its order by 6,000 copies a day, pagination was reduced from 12 to eight pages, the editorial staff was cut from 40 to 28 and the paper faced an annual loss of income of £400,000. Advertising space is not likely to sell well in a paper experiencing troubled times. And if advertisers don't support the paper . . .

The popular papers have less need to rely on advertising revenue than have their more serious competitors and regional papers have a higher proportion of direct, i.e. non-agency, advertising. Even so almost 90% of advertising comes not directly from the big newspaper companies themselves but from agencies. These companies carry out the vital work of researching the potential profitability of placing advertisements and the purchase of advertising space. The agencies depend for their fees on the success of their work, i.e. readership response to the ads they place, which is carefully monitored. If the agencies don't get it right then they, as well as their newspaper customers, will suffer and next time the customers will use another agency. So a good agency, keen to satisfy and retain the folk who pay their bills, will have done a great deal of professional research and taken pains to ensure that their advertisements will be put before the eyes of readers most likely to buy their services or products. Advertisements for jobs, property and cars are the big earners, so premium rates for these generally apply to advertising spaces in prominent positions on the paper: the front page, the first right-hand page (which a reader tends to see first on opening the paper) and the first motoring advertisement in any particular issue.

Knowing the importance of accurate research (and aware that the viability of their companies depends on their accuracy), agencies have their facts and figures coldly cut-and-dried to work on a scrupulous placing of where we all fit into today's society. They've assessed what sort of people the readers of any particular newspaper will be and the advertisements they place will reflect that estimated socio-economic class. Of course they realise that not all readers fall into the same group in every respect; there will always be left-wing supporters reading traditional right-wing papers and die-hard traditionalists liking left-wing titles – so the best that even advertising agencies can do is aim at a general assessment of readership.

Free papers are most dependent on selling advertising space; it is their sole source of income and few can survive for long if their advertising departments fail to generate adequate income. But they can target readership more accurately and may respond to revenue difficulties more quickly and with greater versatility than paid-for local weeklies in the same areas.

Notwithstanding the power of advertising, there are strictly controlled parameters to which agencies and newspapers must adhere. The Advertising Standards Authority (itself funded by a levy on display advertisements) exists to promote and enforce high standards in all non-broadcast advertisements. It is able to act independently of the newspaper industry and the government, and its remit is to ensure that advertisements are 'legal, decent, honest and truthful'. When these high standards are flouted in the case of mail-order, dissatisfied customers may obtain redress with the help of the National Newspaper Mail Order Protection Scheme (MOPS), which also covers their supplements and any inserted material they may carry. The Scheme's office is at 18a King Street, Maidenhead SL6 1EF *tel* 01628 641930 *fax* 01628 637112 *email* enquiries@mops.org.uk

Watchdogs

Leading newspapers have their own ombudsmen whose job it is to cope with complaints from the public. The fact that ombudsmen are appointed by editors themselves fails to assure critics of their impartiality. Their appointments are part of a new Code of Conduct signed by almost all national papers. Of course ombudsmen are people of considerable experience in journalism and – like their counterparts in other fields – need considerable reserves of patience and understanding. But it is hard to see how they can easily ignore their undoubted conflict of interests.

There is seldom a shortage of complaints being lobbied against the press and they come in all guises from complainants large and small, public and private. Complaints about the contents of newspapers and the way they behave are dealt with by the Press Complaints Commission and occasionally writers, particularly freelances, find the code of fair play on their side. In February 2002 a complaint against the *Dorking Advertiser* was upheld when a review of a local restaurant, headlined 'Skullduggery over a butterscotch tart', included a photograph clearly showing a man dining with a companion. This, the man complained, was taken and published without his consent and was in breach of Clause 4 (Harassment) of the Code of Practice. The paper did apologise for any distress that may have been caused but contended that a café was a public place – as any member of the public had a right of free entry – and therefore that the complainant had no reasonable expectation of privacy. Freelances beware!

It is worth noting that dubious advertisers who should be the subject of complaint sometimes lurk in the pages of newspapers: perhaps someone is in the process of such lurking as I write. A few advertisers try to get rich through dishonest dealings with honest, if naïve, writers. While there are some *bona fide* organisations offering to help writers with tutorials and workshops, one offending advertiser promised what he called 'press cards' to buyers of his material. These were described as 'genuine accredited press passes to open many doors and provide many advantages'. Buyers ('Save money and be treated like a VIP!') were also offered windscreen stickers

('Why pay for parking?') and business cards 'recognised by local and international police forces and most authorities worldwide'. For these and other associated goodies, buyers paid £400 for two years, £600 for five years or £1,000 for life ownership. Anyone, including you or me on our home computers, can print out smart 'official' cards: don't be fooled.

. . . And how they do it

The NUJ publishes an official Code of Conduct for its members. This is accepted among a wide spread of journalists and writers in many fields as a fair and sound guide to how writers, staff and freelances alike, should behave. These are its tenets and we should observe and support them (I print its exact, if grammatically flawed, text):

1. The highest professional and ethical standards
2. The defence of press freedom
3. Fair and accurate reporting
4. The rights of reply and corrections
5. The use of straightforward means to obtain information
6. The avoidance of intrusion into private grief and distress
7. The protection of sources
8. A refusal to accept bribes or to allow other inducements to influence the performance of professional duties
9. There shall be no distortion because of advertising
10. There shall be no discrimination against minorities or social groups
11. There shall be no private advantage from information gained in the course of work
12. There shall be no endorsement of commercial products

Years ago the advent of television was thought by some to herald the death of newspapers. In fact the very reverse has proved to be the case: the vast amount of paper used as newsprint has varied little over the past 80 years. If you made a roll 80 centimetres wide and wound it round the globe 30,000 times, you might have enough to supply all the newspapers printed in the United Kingdom in a single year. Newspapers are very much alive and kicking.

Take every opportunity to learn about newspaper production and who does what – to marvel at the whole process. And every time it's done and the paper is ultimately printed, it all has to be done again, perhaps the very next day. A miracle of expertise, enterprise and technology awaits readers for just a few pence – and freelances are an important part of it.

'Lost, yesterday, somewhere between sunrise and sunset, two golden hours, each set with sixty diamond minutes. No reward is offered for they are gone forever.' Horace Mann, 1796–1859 (the first great American advocate of public education)

3. Marketing

For freelance writers for newspapers it is the marketing, the selling of your work, that is the measure of your success.

For all their apparent stability and the long tradition of the industry, newspapers are sobered by the realisation that they are still, and always will be, the servants rather than the masters of the people. Just like provincial and local papers, all national papers are in private ownership, which means that there is no direct government control or restraint; virtually all are financially independent from any political masters. No government subsidies support commercial papers and at the time of writing there is no tax concession apart from the exemption from Value Added Tax on sales. With the cover price often paying for only a small proportion of the huge costs involved, newspaper publishing is virtually all paid for by advertising. Readers pay the cover prices but advertisers pay an enormous annual bill – currently a figure in excess of six billion pounds.

Per head of population we read more newspapers than any other country in the world. How we manage to do so is partly luck in that we are small enough to allow all our national newspapers to be distributed around Britain on a single day. But also, more importantly, we have a great assortment of newspapers in healthy competition with each other which ensures that there is something to satisfy everyone. The provincial press vastly overshadows the nationals and local papers are rooted in the population's affections. There's never any shortage of newspapers to read – or to write for – and the world of newspapers is constantly changing. Nothing stays the same for long.

Newspapers don't issue guidelines to freelances so a careful study of the market is essential. Many writers regard this as a bore. Oh, if only the right market presented itself to us without any fuss or hassle! Unfortunately we all know that it doesn't. Some writers set aside a specific week or day for marketing, saying this does not interfere with their normal writing pattern. However you do it (and it must be done), here are some helpful steps to pain-free marketing:

- Keep a notebook to hand everywhere you might find yourself reading anything; publications that you might not think of as being proper market guides (*see* end of chapter) can refer to what might turn out to be potentially useful markets.
- Make a list of markets you just might want to write for in the future, even if you do not have a particular piece in mind just now.
- Keep a list of alternative markets for your copy, should it be rejected the first time you submit it. (Although this flies in the face of the notion that each paper is unique in what it is looking for, it might not be too long a task to rewrite your piece to suit an alternative market.) Having a second or third market ready to take your work saves time in starting to look again from scratch.
- Keep track of editorial changes, especially among staff with whom you have previously communicated – even if you have not made a sale. Features editors and their staff come and go, and it is a mistake to submit copy or a letter to someone who is no longer on the staff. It looks very unprofessional.
- Keep back-copies of papers you want to write for. Yes, I know they get out of date, but as long as you keep reasonably on top of the back-issues you will find them helpful in reminding you of style, layout and readers' preferences – none of which frequently change.

Almost always do your market study before writing your copy. I say 'almost always' because there are times when this rule may not be appropriate. It is sometimes useful to have copy half-written before doing market study – just awaiting the final touch is a very helpful state to be in. Half-written semi-ready copy may be useful in the cupboard, but beware of filling the cupboard with it.

Local papers

One of the fascinating revelations about visiting a part of the country hitherto unknown to us is that the people are *different*. They may speak a different language or dialect, they dress differently, cook different foods, and have different customs and manners. Above all, they *think* differently. While this is more apparent the further afield we go, it is also true of folk who may live only a few miles away. Pick up a local paper in an area you have never visited before and it will not mean much to you. It reads as if it is talking to a friend, or a few thousand friends, as indeed it is. We have no difficulty in making casual conversation with our acquaintances about titbits of what's happening in the area, scraps of gossip and chatter of mutual interest, but while we remain strangers we feel totally distanced from it. We speak of 'getting to know the place' when we move from our old familiar surroundings, and nothing needs more 'getting to know' than the local paper – if we plan to sell to it. And what we as writers are really 'getting to know', of course, is the readers. We have to know who they are and how they think before we can write for them.

A local weekly paper is a good starting-point and for many people this will be where they gain early success. Never belittle your own work when you sell to these markets and to 'free' papers; the word 'provincial' has no place here wearing its condescending hat. Weeklies are as important a part of the whole newspaper industry as are any of their mass-circulation daily and regional cousins. Local papers are exactly what they intend to be: something to relax with, good friends until consigned to their afterlife of lining the wheelie-bin or the cat's litter-tray. Before that inglorious end they usually stay around for a while and the contributor whose work can survive repeated study by what is often a personally involved and severely critical readership is doing very well indeed.

Whatever else local papers may be they are all intensely local in appeal. As you study them more closely you will realise that 'local' does not mean 'narrow-minded' or 'parochial' in its pejorative sense. Broadly speaking, such papers exist for three reasons: to strengthen community 'togetherness', with pride in past or current achievements, to protect the community by highlighting particular shortcomings, in local street-lighting, say, or by allowing readers to voice protests about local issues, and (perhaps most importantly of the three) to inform their readers. It almost goes without saying they must also interest and should frequently entertain them as well.

Because there are so many of them local papers are the hardest to list. It's virtually impossible to detail what they want from freelance writers, yet of all the newspaper markets they present the easiest target. You may be weary of the old advice 'Study the market' but writing for local papers proves just how essential this is. If you are genuinely interested in your chosen area you will find this market study painless – you may even be unaware that you are doing it. Read your local paper regularly and you can hardly help but get the 'feel' of it; you'll soon understand how its mind works and you'll know what the reaction of the people who are reading it will be to its various parts. You could call this absorption or instinct, rather than market study. However it's described it is this depth of knowing a market that shows you what and how to write for it.

To find out which local papers are published in an area new to you just keep watch over newspaper births and deaths (and sometimes marriages) in local and provincial journalism. Any local library should be able to tell you what is published to cover your area or the area you are interested in but a more practical way of finding the very latest in local publishing is to ask a newsagent. Make a friend of him and waylay him for a chat at a time when he's not busy. He'll probably be delighted to find someone who is sufficiently interested in newspapers to ask about them. If nothing else, a close notebook-in-hand study of his shelves will give you all the local information you need about what is published in the area.

The glue that holds these papers high in people's affections is their intensely *local* interest. They are read by people of all backgrounds and levels of education, with varying likes and dislikes, but by just about everyone in the community. The local paper speaks for us all. We feel comfortable with it, although we may sometimes curse what we read in its pages, because it represents familiar territory – things and people we know about and *home*.

Free papers

Gone are the days when free newspapers were considered too humble to write for; now, with few exceptions, they've pulled up their socks and worked hard to make themselves worthy of everyone's market study.

In the United Kingdom we can expect (and often cannot avoid) something like 46 million free papers pushed through our letterboxes at regular intervals. More than half of them are free 'extras' from the same stables as our paid-for weeklies, which is perhaps why the business of issuing both is known to the trade as 'total publishing'. These freesheets, as we call them, vary greatly in size, quality and frequency of publication, although most are weeklies. Free papers are read by about 75% of all adults (compared to 45% reading paid-for papers) and offer many openings for freelance writers. Where the paid-for weeklies will have established correspondents in most circulation areas, freesheets largely depend on the man/woman-in-the-street for a supply of news, coverage of forthcoming events, topical and non-topical features – and whatever else the enterprising writer may create. Therein lies a freelance's opportunity. A glance at any freesheet page will readily reveal openings to the market-seeking eye of a determined contributor; closer careful study and some resourceful work will be the first steps to supplying what is wanted. Incidentally, as the idea has died that writing for freesheets is beneath the 'real' journalist's dignity, so has the rumour that 'frees don't pay'; nowadays most of them do. Freesheets are big business and of course their contributors should and do expect to be treated as 'proper' writers.

National papers

In journalists' parlance 'regional' papers are morning dailies with large circulations covering wide areas, like the *Yorkshire Post*, the *Birmingham Post* or the *Western Daily Press* and their Sunday equivalents. Local weekly or evening papers are generally described as 'provincial' papers.

UK national papers fall into three broad categories. The *Sun* and the *Mirror*, fierce 'red-top' competitors, head the morning popular field. The appeal of the top-selling tabloids relies on content and approach, the emphasis being on human-interest and sensational stories (especially in the world of showbiz), sport and unpretentious light-hearted family entertainment. The tabloids report in more condensed or shortened versions than the heavier papers and offer many more illustrations. Tabloid Sundays generally adopt the same pattern as their daily counterparts.

The middle-market tabloids, the *Daily Mail* and the *Express*, are rather more upmarket with a very different readership. At the top of the morning quality papers sit *The Times* and the *Telegraph*, the latter greatly out-selling the former and appealing to a higher taste and to readers with a more leisured, free-spending lifestyle. The quality papers take a serious view of the news, supporting it with informed analysis and comment on political, economic, social and world events – news and comment being kept firmly apart. The arts, business, entertainment, sport, finance, women's affairs, employment and leisure pages feature in all, and leader pages reflect a paper's editorial policy and tone. Sunday qualities follow much the same style and most publish several sections and/or colour magazines, the assumption being that at the weekends the nation has more time for seriously digesting the state of the world, with leisure topics taking a prominent place. Competition is strong, so much so that some nationals publish their big-size papers on Saturdays to forestall the traditional Sunday bulkies.

As I write there are 24 daily papers published in the UK. Some of them have regional or city coverage, but most of them are truly 'national' papers, in that they can be bought virtually anywhere in the country. Circulation figures vary widely: the *Sun* sells 3.5 million copies a day; the *Independent* less than quarter of a million; the *London Evening Standard* sells fewer than half a million (perhaps it is London's 'local paper'?) and the *Scotsman* sells some 78,000 copies per day. All these figures are the latest given by the Audit Bureau of Circulation. The adult – aged 15+ – population of the UK is estimated as between 46 and 47 million although it changes every day. Occasionally nationals and big-circulation regional papers publish special issues for promoting particular events or to attract specific readers, but on the whole they keep to their mainstream purposes: serving the interest of their daily readers buying in their hundreds of thousands or millions.

Sunday papers are equally vibrant. More than 26 million of us read one every weekend notwithstanding their range of supplements – those half-paper-half-magazine publications which offer golden opportunities in their own right for diligent and market-conscious freelances – threatens to overwhelm the household. Just one Sunday edition of a typical broadsheet can carry more information than an educated person 300 years ago could read in a lifetime. Other supplements are published with the big nationals on any day of the week in an attempt to keep ahead of the major Sunday issues – some on Thursdays and many on Saturdays. *The Sunday Times*, for example, issues supplements on culture, style, money and business, as well as its own *Sunday Times Magazine*. Education, computer-help, job-finding, fashion, general information and life itself; for whatever interests readers, there's a supplement. And whatever interests readers interests *us* as writers. Of course circulation figures do not reflect the number of *readers*, as the majority of papers sold are read by more than one person. We can safely multiply circulation figures by 50% to estimate the actual number of readers.

When we look at nationals it is plain that the differences between them (with special exceptions) lie not in the location of the readership, but in what advertisers call 'reader-classification'. The *Sun* and *The Times* can be bought in Kent as in Lancashire, so it is the papers themselves that have done their own market study; in general terms, the *Sun* does not attract the same readers as does *The Times* and (as with all papers) both are produced to appeal to a band of readers whose likes and dislikes, and therefore buying-tastes, they know and understand. We must do the same. Whatever market we write for, success demands that we know the readers before we begin to write for them.

The provincial press

The huge provincial press thrives on regional and local events. The nationals concentrate on national and international news flooding in from correspondents, news agencies and other sources. But should an important news story break in its circulation area, a local paper will of course give the story closer coverage than national papers can – and the supporting features relevant to the story will be of enormous interest to local readers. But how, you may ask, is the freelance to be prepared for, say, an unidentified body being found on a deserted moorland site, a local child winning a national ballet competition or a fishing smack missing for days from a local harbour? Noting the differences in the way that national, regional and local papers cover the same event – perhaps a major disaster – is rewarding market study in itself. If it's a story of more than local importance it ought to be you who writes it up for the regional paper as well – and perhaps gives at least a tip-off to a national paper. With adequate research (and speed) you will have all the facts ready at your fingertips, you will know the area and be able to contact the people involved.

Reader identification

So who are all these readers? How much do we need to know about them? How much do they earn, what are their jobs, what are their future prospects, what do they spend their money on, where do they go for holidays? Advertising pundits know the answers and we can profit from their experience and know-how at their expense. Study adverts closely to discover the readers *they* are aiming at. Phone the advertising department and ask them to send you a media pack. If they demur, tell them you're a freelance wanting to write for the paper. If they won't or don't send you a pack you have lost nothing.

Professional readership analysis is conducted in complex detail by the National Readership Survey, a limited company set up on behalf of the newspaper, magazine and advertising industries (*see* page 41 for contact details). Random but highly controlled sampling is taken from the electoral roll. All questions relate to the chief wage-earner or the head of the household. The most recently published NRS report provides readership estimates for 12 national dailies, 14 Sunday papers and 37 national newspaper supplements.

In many walks of life modern classification functions by postal code – which is not always to our advantage. Disturbing tales are sometimes told of people being denied specific help in housing, for example, or health care or schooling for their children – because they happen to live in the 'wrong' postcode area. The National Readership Survey selects domestic addresses at random, regardless of postal codes. All interviews take place in the respondents' homes, and on average take 30 minutes. Against this background readers are categorised in the following proportions:

A	Higher managerial, administrative or professional	3.2%
B	Intermediate managerial, administrative or professional	14.2%
C1	Supervisory or clerical, and junior managerial, administrative or professional	24.7%
C2	Skilled manual workers	27.1%
D	Semi-skilled and unskilled manual workers	17.3%
E	Unclassified i.e. below any classification level, state pensioners or widows, casual or lowest grade workers and unemployed	13.5%

We were all readers before we became writers, and it is by becoming readers again – this time analytical, observant and thoughtful readers – that we become better writers. I cannot overemphasise the importance of *knowing* your readers. Try to imagine them reading your work. If you know anyone who regularly buys your targeted title you are already at an advantage.

Who owns what

The largest 20 regional press publishers now account for 84% of all regional press titles and 96% of total weekly circulation, including the six free regional morning titles. Heading the list is Trinity Mirror plc with 234 titles spreading from Aberdeen to Plymouth. Newsquest (Media Group) Ltd comes next in ranking, followed by Northcliffe Newspapers Group Ltd, Johnston Press plc and Associated Newspapers Ltd. Between them they publish 782 newspapers. Altogether the top 20 regional press publishers churn out 1,072 papers printing almost 69 million copies. As many of the giants' empires also include international commercial involvement – in television, communications, shipping, property, airlines, oil, insurance and high-level commerce, for example – tremendous power in the world of communications rests in their hands. The huge power of newspaper chains has long been a major factor in British journalism and anxiety about too much being controlled by the same proprietor surfaces every time there is a newspaper merger or one swallows up another.

The most powerful giant is News Corporation which promotes itself as 'producing and distributing the most compelling news, information and entertainment to the farthest reaches of the globe'. This is Rupert Murdoch's empire which includes the *Sun*, the *News of the World*, *The Times* (and all its supplements), the *Sunday Times*, *Twentieth Century Fox*, *Harper Collins Publishers*, the *Australian*, *Sky*, *Star*, the *New York Post*, and a host of radio and television stations, film studios and other media enterprises all over the world.

As I write, a new UK Communications Bill is being discussed whereby large newspaper groups may override the existing restrictions confining their empires. This cannot be in the best interests of small publishers at the foot of the tree – there are 45 small publishers who produce just one title each. Your local paper may be run by one man and his dog, or it may be just a very small cog in a huge business machine.

Looking further afield: overseas markets

You don't have to buy copies of all the papers you want to study (although you may prefer to do so) or even squint as best you can while they're on the newsagent's shelves. Several online services not only supply lists of what papers exist but also give you the opportunity of reading them online. Be aware that most online versions are not exactly the same as their printed siblings but contain extracts from them and sometimes additions to them. These include local papers in the UK and in many other countries (yes, every local paper is somebody's favourite) as well as nationals, regionals and specialist papers all over the world, published in English as well as in their native tongues. We writers are not confined to UK markets, for the rest of the world is open to any freelance who can write what is wanted. Newspaper publishers in the United States estimate that eight out of ten adult Americans read a newspaper every day – and there is a similar picture to be drawn in many developed nations.

If you could read all the different newspapers (and there are many thousands) you would find them as varied as the people who read them. News, background stories and interesting items may be their staple fare but there is a fascinating extra dimension about newspapers. They are not just inky words and pictures printed on greyish-white paper; in a sense all their own, newspapers are alive. In their pages you can expect to read about the events of the day, covering anything and everything from changes at a local factory and a fire in a city library to the illness of an international footballer, the financial crisis of an orchestral company and the latest gyrations of international personalities. All is grist to the mill.

The Communist Party *People's Daily*, for example, is the most influential and authoritative newspaper in China. Printed in English as well as in Chinese, it brings its readers the latest news dispatches from the Chinese government as well as major domestic news and international news releases. It reflects the views of the Chinese people, expounds on justice and lambasts various forms of malpractice. *The Jakarta Post* is the largest English newspaper in Indonesia. A daily, it offers breaking news and a wealth of information on Indonesia. *Ha'aretz* is an Israeli independent daily newspaper (except Saturdays) taking a broadly liberal outlook both on domestic issues and on international affairs. With a journalistic staff of some 330 reporters, writers and editors, it plays an important role in the shaping of public opinion and is read with care in government and decision-making circles.

Get into the habit of looking for markets and you will find they pop up everywhere. Milk your research to use all the outlets you can find; a once-only sale is fine, but selling the same idea – albeit in different words – several times is better and more profitable.

Syndication

Syndication is another way of finding new markets for your already published material. Here and overseas it can continue to earn smaller sums for writers ready to hand their work over to syndication agencies. Syndication is not only possible but ethically acceptable and its secret is that many newspapers have clearly defined and limited circulation areas. So an editor in Aberdeen won't be at all worried if you have sold the article he's buying to another editor in Penzance because nobody in the Aberdeen circulation area would see newspapers published in Penzance. For the same reason the Penzance editor won't be annoyed at publication in distant Aberdeen, even if he ever gets to hear about it. If an Aberdeen reader, by chance visiting Penzance (or vice versa), reads what he already read in last week's paper at home, he will only feel a slight superiority that his home paper 'got there first', and no harm is done to either title.

All the same, if copy is being syndicated – i.e. has already been sold at least once elsewhere – you should indicate that this is so to any editor you offer it to. The fact that it has already met with approval somewhere else is likely to commend it to him: it's of proven marketable quality. He also knows that it won't cost him as much as would non-syndicated copy, since you expect to be paid for it several times.

In this type of marketing a query letter is essential. Use it to introduce yourself (briefly) and your wares (more fully) to newspaper editors in widely differing parts of the country. Freesheets buy a huge amount of syndicated material. It's a good idea to consult a marketing guide (*see* pp. 40–42) to study where newspaper groups may mean that circulation areas overlap; purchase by a group may involve passing your copy to several titles within the group. Who would guess, for example, that papers in Portsmouth and Sunderland are under the same umbrella? Cautious research into other titles and the groups they belong to can prevent you from making a blunder.

Because the fee for individual sales will be modest, it is not cost-effective to try syndicating work that doesn't have a better-than-average chance of being accepted. Maybe it's the humble reward that has given syndication a poor image. But weigh up the advantages: each payment is only part of what the copy may earn in its lifetime, there is no extra research or writing to be done, and the expense you incur with each submission is small. Photocopying your piece and writing a short covering letter to recipients have been the only work; envelopes and postage the total cost. You could call syndication 'money for jam'. It is particularly easy if you have a large stock of useful copy (despatch a dozen or more items together for maximum impact and minimum trouble) and don't mind the jam being rather thinly spread on each piece.

Easy – but is it worth it? Maybe, if it can be accomplished as well as other useful work, not instead of it. You might prefer to let someone else do the work of syndication for you. There are many agencies and some only take freelance copy. Their usual terms are a 50/50 split on all sales. The leading agencies may state that they're looking for professional writers with 'international minds', and most operate on a basic 20–25% handling charge. They will probably send lists of ideas provided by their contributors to editors. The paper might then take up several ideas and want further details. As this happens the agency (taking its share of any fee going) might pass your copy onto another agency. It's big business at this level and so are the slices taken from the rewards. At the click of a keyboard what started as a £250 fee can shrink by 50% of 50% less deductions for this and that – and reach you as just £20. Think carefully before deciding whether syndication is worth it or not.

Marketing help

Published writers who've 'been there, done that' can stop you from making the same mistakes as they did and may be able to save you a great deal of time. Marketing advice from anyone anywhere is always valuable – but I do urge you to corroborate it yourself. Word of mouth often provides valuable information about markets you may not have heard about. There are small newspapers for many specialist concerns and new ones are frequently born, while others fade away. Their readers may engage in unusual sports, be lovers of rare pets or sufferers from uncommon diseases; discovering these outlets provides welcome opportunities for the freelance writer. In general conversation people talk about what their friends and relatives do. But be careful. Hints from other folk, however well-meant, may be out-of-date or inappropriate, the helper not understanding what you are writing or wish to write. Such advice, never to be scorned, is better seen as nothing more than a signpost. Early in my writing life when I was desperate to find a market for some copy I especially liked (my self-satisfaction should have warned me) a friend recommended a particular paper with the encouragement, 'Oh, they'll take anything.' Not, perhaps, what she meant to say; they still didn't take mine. Always do your own research on markets while being grateful to anyone who points you in the right direction.

Delve into the background of the paper you wish to write for. Find out who owns it (and its associated titles; few papers exist on their own) and get to know the editor's personal likes and dislikes, as well as the company or title policy on what will be included in its pages. Keep track of editorial changes; your current information may have been superseded by a change of editorship. Most papers don't announce such changes in their pages so you must keep your wits about you. If in doubt, or if your previous information is old, ring the switchboard and ask for the editor's name. The more you know the better equipped you are to make your arrows hit the target. Doing this extra market research always pays dividends.

Over and over again I have proved that nothing is more successful than finding markets for yourself. Catch them in their infancy – experience and experimentation will sometimes tell you how viable they may be in the long term – and you've a good chance not only of 'getting in on the ground floor' but also of persuading the editor to mould the paper just a little in the way you would like it to go. Always watch out for news of papers about to be launched and think of ways in which you can contribute to them. Does your head instantly fill with ideas for regular features, articles, original columns, or – at the very least – query letters to the editor? And does excitement mount as you get started on them? Even if it doesn't when you first start writing for newspapers, as in every other craft, practice makes perfect – and it soon will.

You can always rely on the established market guides to point you in the right direction. Bear in mind that most of them are published annually and may not be right up-to-date so you will have to do your own checking to discover if the given facts and figures (addresses, phone numbers, editors and so on) have changed since the guides were published. Such sources as these are well known and open to all writers so competition for the markets mentioned in their pages may be stiff. Most have internet sites where the latest information may be found.

- *Writers' & Artists' Yearbook* (A & C Black Ltd, 37 Soho Square, London W1D 3QZ *tel* 0207 758 0200 *email* sales@acblack.com *website* http://www.acblack.com)
  Recommended by the Society of Authors, this long-established *vade-mecum* is in two main sections: markets, and general information for writers.
- *Willings Press Guide* (Chess House, 34 Germain Street, Bucks HP5 1SJ *tel* 0870 736 0010 *website* www.willingspress.com)
  Firmly established as the most accurate, comprehensive and up-to-date media guide available. Now in its 129th edition and containing over 50,000 entries, it targets specific titles in the UK and worldwide with up-to-date editorial contact information. It is available in two printed volumes covering the UK and the rest of the world, or online, giving at-a-glance access to the world's media. Costing £190 (each) for Volume 1 (United Kingdom) and Volume 2 (International) at the time of writing, it may be found in most reference libraries.
- *Benn's Media* is produced each year in three separate volumes covering different parts of the world: UK, Europe, and (rest of) World. Each volume is available separately, at £152 per volume or £345 for all three volumes. Here are all the newspapers in the UK, both national and regional, with circulation details, key management, editorial and advertisement executives. Cover prices and advertising rates are also listed. It is available in some public libraries or from the publisher CMP Information Ltd, Riverbank House, Angel Lane, Tonbridge, Kent TN9 1SE *tel* 01732 362666.
- *BRADgroup* (British Rate and Data), 33–39 Bowling Green Lane, London EC1R 0DA *tel* 020 7505 8281 *fax* 020 7505 8264 *website* www.intellagencia.com/productlist.asp.
  Known in the business as 'BRAD', this provides updated rates and data on over 13,000 media entries across all sectors. Circulation and audience-reach figures in each entry allow easy comparison with other titles in the market. It probably remains the UK's most reliable guide to circulation figures and readership profiles. The newspaper births and

deaths section is also invaluable. Even when you've identified and located regional and local papers you can't relax; papers close, change their titles, disappear within their own groups or merge with former rivals.

Internet market guides

Help in locating markets abounds on the internet. Please note, however, that this method of finding markets is often little more than just that – *finding* them and being aware that they exist. Obtain from these sites details of the areas they cover, statistics about editors, addresses and telephone numbers etc. only as a starting point. Many papers have their online equivalents to show you but these are not substitutes for the hard copies; online editions are not necessarily the same as their printed siblings, even though they may cover the same new items, sports results and some other features.

The following organisations may also be helpful:

- National Readership Survey (NRS Ltd), 42 Drury Lane, London WC2B 5RT *tel* 020 7632 2915 *fax* 020 7632 2916 *website* www.nrs.co.uk
  A non-profit-making organisation providing readership estimates for virtually all UK newspapers and consumer magazines.
- The Newspaper Society, Bloomsbury House, 74–77 Great Russell Street, London WC1B 3DA *tel* 020 7636 7014 *fax* 020 7631 5119 *website* www.newspapersoc.org.uk
  The voice of Britain's regional and local press and the country's second-largest advertising medium, read by 84% of UK adults. Members publish around 1,300 daily, weekly, paid-for and free titles across the UK.
- Internet Public Library Newspapers *website* www.ipl.org/reading/news/
  Excellent index of national and local newspapers covering Africa, Asia, the Caribbean, Central America, Europe, the Middle East, South America, Canada, Mexico, the South Pacific and the United States.
- Britain in the USA *website* www.britain-info.org/media_review
  A daily review of British media, prepared by the BBC.

- ThePaperBoy.com *website* www.thepaperboy.com
  American Ian Duckworth opened this site in November 1997 to satisfy his craving for easy access to quality news: a useful resource with links to worldwide newspapers.
- Audit Bureau of Circulations, Saxon House, 211 High Street, Berkhamsted, Hertfordshire HP4 1AD *tel* 01442 870800, *fax* 01442 200700 *email* marketing@abc.org.uk
  Launched in 1931, in response to advertiser demand for independent verification of the claims made by the advertising sales teams of newspapers and magazines – especially the national press (then known as Fleet Street).

Submissions: the query letter

Most editors prefer to discuss an idea first so that they can help mould it and perhaps offer useful leads. This is to the writer's advantage as well as the editor's, so always be ready to co-operate with any suggestions offered. The old adage is still valid: the editor is always right! So opening your sales technique with a query letter is still the best way – usually. If you happen to know your editor or have already sold to his paper, an initial phone call may be more appropriate. But random phone calls can prove poor starters: the editor and his staff just might be extra busy when you call and your message could sit on an underling's desk as nothing more than a few scribbled words until the cleaners find it a week later. A similar fate may befall emailed copy or queries. Such queries may get put through to the editor who does not want to be interrupted at that moment, and your earlier cordial relationship may be cut with a terse response.

An initial letter to an editor is not something to be dashed off in a hurry. It can often mark the first point of your sale: you are selling yourself as a contributor whom he will value. The letter should be flawlessly printed or typed (*never* hand-written) on good quality headed paper: first impressions do count – and even if the only person to see your envelope is the editor's secretary, they still count. If the secretary leaves his mail on his desk for him to open she will invariably arrange it with the *smallest* envelope on top; so by putting your query letter in a big bold envelope you may not be doing yourself a favour.

Queries should be succinct, easy to read and preferably not spread beyond a single sheet: no rambling, nothing extraneous. Reveal your particular qualifications to write on this topic and any special sources you can tap. Your letter should indicate your approach as well as your proposed tone and style. A very short opening sentence might be appropriate. Make your point at the beginning and provide a brief resumé of your background experience only as relevant to the piece you are trying to sell. Don't be bashful about revealing your published work to date; nobody else will help you sell your copy – we freelances work alone and have to speak up for ourselves. List facts, not wishes, and add a 'hook' to let the editor know you are up-to-date with his paper and what might be just what he needs for an early issue. But don't get carried away. Offering to supply or hinting that you *might* be able to supply something you are not sure you *can* provide could lead to trouble later.

When you've written your letter put it away for a few days before reading it anew. Does it look professional? Does it grab the editor's attention, telling him you know what you're talking about and can deliver the goods – on time? Will it satisfy him that you are a contributor he can do business with, i.e. discuss particular points in the copy without hassle? (You'd be surprised how many beginners offer editors their work and refuse to alter a word, considering it sacrosanct.) Does your letter give all the important and relevant points, and nothing irrelevant? Is it polite but not obsequious? If you offer to phone him when he's had time to read it (generally more appropriate on local papers) remember there's a fine line between business-like persistence and being a nuisance.

Follow-up calls

Meet your chosen editor face to face if you can. He might not like such contact, even after an introductory query letter from you, but if he does a meeting will be invaluable to you. Assuming that you have something he wants (and that is always the inescapable criterion) it will be harder for him to reject it when meeting you in person. If your idea involves a regular column or something more than a single one-off piece, he may ask you to his office to discuss it. Prepare with care, taking with you all the papers that you might need – in the right order for easy reference. Be relaxed and let him do the talking until he asks questions. And when he does, keep your replies short and to the point. He knows what he wants, he will have seen countless freelances before you offering their wares and he is probably sizing you up. Finally, always remember the 'three Ps': Polite Persistence Pays (other writers I know add a couple more: Professionalism and Productivity).

'*The secret to selling your writing is to understand your buyers and what they need.*' Dan Poynter (American professor and author of more than 70 books for writers)

4. What to Write

Courses in creative writing sometimes urge their students to think of half-a-dozen worthwhile ideas and write an opening paragraph about each, at this stage ignoring style, punctuation etc. (That last instruction would bother me as I can't let visual errors sit on the page or screen in front of me without tidying them up as I work – but you may not share my funny little ways.) Then, the tutors suggest, write what the story is about and how you will be tackling it, followed by a summary of the information you will need and your intended research methods.

While this is not bad advice to get you going, ideas that have only come when forced are never so malleable or happy as those arriving in your head out of thin air. For this reason lists of ideas may merely stultify writers before they begin. And if everyone has or can read the same list, finding original slants on the ideas provided is harder, not easier. 'Nothing has yet been said that's not been said before,' said the Roman comic dramatist Terence (c. 195–159 BC).

Is that so? How do the best ideas come? What pundits now call 'brainstorming' lets one idea lead to another and sometimes ends up far removed from the original put in your head by other people. For a long time I wasn't sure what was meant by the term 'lateral thinking' until I realised I'd been doing it instinctively all my working life: letting an idea mill round my brain, flop in and out of the subconscious and drift here and there before hitting me in the writing or typing fingers with a stubborn refusal to be ignored. Ah, it would say to me, *this* is what you want to write about next.

By chance I heard of *The Busman's Prayer*, a parody of *The Lord's Prayer*, and a favourite poem, of unknown authorship, of disgruntled London bus drivers for the past half-century or more:

Our Father, Who art in Hendon, Harrow Road be thy name.
Thy Kingston come, thy Wimbledon in Erith as it is in Hendon.
Give us this day our Berkhampstead and forgive us our Westminsters
As we who forgive those who Westminster against us.
Lead us not into Temple station and deliver us from Ealing,
For thine is the Kingston, the Purley and the Crawley
For Iver and Esher,
Crouch End.

This led me to search for other variations, not only according to different routes, but also for other occupations. I couldn't imagine bus drivers were the only folk with such imagination – and in due course I was able to write a humourous piece about versions of *The Lord's Prayer* for dustmen, postmen and deliverymen, among others.

A long drive in heavy traffic with much crawling along set me musing on the strange messages that some folk put in the back windows of their cars. 'Baby on board' is functional but 'I don't like being passed' and 'I'm always in front of you' are more interesting. After four hours of slow driving I had more messages than I needed to fill a small corner in a motoring paper. (It's worth noting that without my trusty voice recorder, which is always on standby wherever I go, I would not have been able to remember them all.)

The old adage 'Write what you know' is sound advice but doesn't always solve the difficulty of not knowing enough about any one thing to write about it. It is important to feel at ease with whatever you are writing. If *you* are not enjoying the writing of it, why should other people enjoy reading it? Most of us endure the same domestic and trivial experiences – so how do you deal with them? Write about it. Explain how you cope with common aggravations and situations, maybe in an amusing piece. Better still, write about *uncommon* human experiences and you'll be surprised (when you start your research) to find that quite a lot of other people share them. For example, I overheard a man on a train telling a friend how he gave his wife a real shock just by rubbing his feet on the carpet. 'She's surprised because you wipe your feet?' queried the friend. 'No,' came the reply, 'rubbing my feet on the floor fills me with so much static electricity I only have to touch her and she leaps in the air.' This led me to wonder how many other people are so affected by such an over-charge and what effect it might have on their lives. How does it happen? What is the scientific explanation, in lay terms? How could this be put to good use – or bad – and is it an asset or a disadvantage?

On another occasion I happened to meet a couple who had met while playing both halves of a pantomime cow. There was much laughter about who was the front and who the rear, which led me to research unusual or amusing circumstances of first meetings. Scan local newspapers and delve into stories, asking local people for further as yet unpublished details. I talk to a wide variety of people just about everywhere I go – and most of them have a story to tell.

Humour is in short supply in newspapers which are often too full of doom and gloom. A friend caught her skirt in the car door when she parked by a major supermarket. No amount of poking and pulling by obliging (and laughing) shoppers could open the car door or free her skirt. She was helpless. How did the story end? (See the solution at the end of this chapter.)

Is it worth burning up petrol just to save pence at the pumps? Do local research about prices at various garages. Your neighbour was stopped for speeding but only got an invitation to attend a remedial course for drivers? Write about it and how others might benefit from it. Be seasonally aware: write about Christmassy things by June or July, and always get a new angle on the old favourites. Set yourself the task of jotting down during a single day, say, five ideas you would like to develop and write about. A young colleague was so determined to train her brain into thinking up good ideas (don't waste your time on ones that are going nowhere) that she started at the beginning of a month with a single idea, then two on the second of the month, and so on. By about the tenth day she realised she had taught her brain well and turned to perfecting the wealth of ideas she already had instead of blocking her head with yet more – for the time being. Yes, that's how idea-finding can take you over if you are not selective and sensible about it. Absolutely everywhere you look, everything you see and hear – there are *hundreds* of good ideas just waiting for you to find and develop. Often you don't even have to look.

Unsuspected by us and without any particular bidding, ideas sit on the doorstep and *demand* to be let in. When this happens to you, welcome them with confidence. Of course they'll be a bit bedraggled and you'll have to work on them, usually very hard. Keep your senses on full alert (which becomes a habit without conscious effort) and your brain in 100% receptive mode. Good ideas are like stray dogs brought in from the cold: all they want is for you to nurture them and fatten them up before sending them to safe homes.

Finding it hard to start writing even when an idea is nagging you, puts you under pressure. Far from being a disadvantage, this can be positively beneficial – since if you want to write for newspapers every piece you write will have a deadline (though it may not be needed urgently). Working to even an artificial deadline shows you how you would cope with a real one; it gets the adrenalin gushing. There's nothing like a deadline to sort the women from the girls.

Specialist columns

Travel, theatre, nature, gardening, reviewing books, films, television, music, fine arts – how do you get these jobs? Before reading any further be sure that you really *want* one; all regular columns involve a major commitment from you and just can't be done well without a good deal of persistent, dedicated work. Daily or weekly spots in newspapers are big eaters of original ideas. They are often the best-read parts of papers, so good columnists are assiduously courted and well paid – but they have to work hard.

Do you fancy being a travel writer? Are you sufficiently disciplined? Would you be ready to accept the restrictions and responsibilities? Professionalism is never more tested than in this job for being a freelance travel writer is far from being a tourist. To you falls the work of research, planning your journey and making all the arrangements – as well as establishing the job on the paper, with all its implications.

Keeping notes (and probably taking pictures) of where you go, whom you talk to and what you do, all done with the object of writing newspaper copy, is not at all like writing chatty letters or postcards to the folks back home.

Of course you will enjoy free travel and accommodation, with many other freebies coming your way, and can work as little or as often as you wish if this arrangement suits your pocket and your editors. Above all, you'll get paid for seeing the world and meeting people you could only dream about otherwise. If you consider the disadvantages minimal compared to the glamorous lifestyle that travel writing can offer, you will need to gather inside information before you begin. How do you find people ready to give you free press trips and how do you introduce yourself to them? Remember your goal is not a sun-drenched beach in Sri Lanka or an all-expenses-paid Caribbean cruise but a space in your selected newspaper – and a good fee. The story you are going to write must be central in your head as you enjoy the perks of a luxurious lifestyle (although some travel writing may be to underdeveloped poverty-stricken countries where the lifestyle is very different). Never lose sight of what your readers will want to know and how you can make them feel they were there with you.

Many freelances vow that there is nothing more satisfying than a regular page/half-page/column/corner all to themselves. This type of work has been one of my specialities for many years and I can vouch for the advantages of it. Usually such an arrangement results from an approach made to an editor by the writer able to show convincing evidence of his ability to hold down a regular place in the paper. It's not a commission won without effort, often over a number of years; the editor will want to know you will be able to sustain an unlimited time at the job, that your copy will constantly be fresh and innovative, and, most importantly, that it will always arrive on time. But when happy about these criteria, many editors are only too glad to hand over responsibility for a portion of the paper and know they needn't worry about it any more.

Letting the editor know your worth by several times selling him other copy is a good basis for asking for a regular column (we'll refer to it as a 'column' even though it may be more or less). In this way you have a chance of impressing him with your efficiency and dedication. On other occasions editors may invite you, out of the blue; but however it begins, a regular column is not something to be accepted lightly. It is hard to build up a good reputation and even harder to live up to it every week, let alone every *day*. Thinking you have a well of ideas that will never run dry is easy; tapping it day after day (or however frequently your column demands you do so) and finding it still full, or full enough, may be different. Fortunately, I've found that wells do have the magic property of being able to refill themselves. It must be that tapping the well of ideas gets the brain filling it up at increasing speed. I must not complain, therefore, because my own regular columns have gradually but inexorably imposed on me an instinctive habit of filling their particular wells even when I no longer want to tap them or at least want a break from doing so. Visiting friends, being on vacation, when ill in hospital, I can't stop the wells filling. (Being a theatre-reviewer, even when I go to a show 'off duty' my mind is soon turning round the intro, shape and viewpoint of review copy.) I hope you can switch your brain off more satisfactorily than I can but if you are a slave to your head then at least you will never run out of ideas. Being an anagram-addict, I invited readers to submit their best ones to a paper – and they did so in their hundreds. This soon turned into a mini-column which ran for a few felicitous weeks. Sorting them out was a task I so enjoyed that I can't resist quoting some of the best: punishment *nine thumps*, a shop-lifter *has to pilfer* and a decimal point *I'm a dot in place*. Ideas hard to find? Not so.

Of equal importance is that your copy must never be late. *Never*? If you are whisked off for unexpected surgery or bereaved of a close family member nobody would expect you to keep up an uninterrupted supply. But relations coming to stay, taking your summer holiday, simply being too busy doing something else; try these as excuses for late copy and your editor won't keep you for long. Of course the same rule applies for all copy, not just regular columns: short of real and rare emergencies, a *deadline must be kept*. The secret of being able to accept deadlines and still sleep at night may be this: plan ahead carefully, know your own writing capacity in terms of the research you may have to do for a particular item and the time it is likely to take you to write it, and (the best safety net) have plenty of copy ready at home in your private store. Keep some ready to file, more half-ready and only waiting for up-to-date material, and yet more awaiting your attention at any time to maintain the quality and quantity of work in the store cupboard.

So what types of regular columns are out there waiting? Their themes are boundless: nature, profiles of famous people, chess, horoscopes, computers, crosswords, competitions, children's and women's pages, young mothers, pop music, pets, food, gardening – anything that interests people will make a good column. Travel, sport, motoring, business and finance are among the topics nearly always covered by staff writers (it's not hard to understand why) and contributions to these sections have to be exceptional, if not unique. Nevertheless, faint heart never won fair lady, despite well-established opposition, so don't fear to try your hand. And if you're not successful at first, remember that every rejection puts you closer to a sale: failure is the mother of invention. Don't give up.

Make use of special knowledge

I love the theatre. If you're passionate about something your enthusiasm will show in your writing – but enthusiasm is not enough. For many topics it is important to have reliable and up-to-date knowledge: write about an old Blackpool theatre without first checking its fortunes in recent years or months and more knowledgeable readers will soon correct me if I'm wrong – to the editor's annoyance and some loss of face for his paper. Better still, find something about your topic that is not generally known, something fascinating, and above all of intense interest and delight to other people who share your obsession. Other writers love the theatre and are also writing about it, so what can I do to make my copy fresher, more provocative, more informative and irresistible? 'A drama critic,' wrote George Bernard Shaw, 'is a man who leaves no turn unstoned.'

If the paper you choose doesn't already run a column on your topic you'll be in a better position than if you just contribute to one already run by somebody else. Regular columns can (and often do) involve you in other fascinating writing jobs. Mine have taken me overseas on promotional tours, made me editor of annuals and introduced me to hundreds of fascinating people. They've also given me more regular columns in other papers here and overseas, and led to more pleasant surprises than I can recall. A column will get you known and your work constantly read and appreciated. There are pleasant by-products too. Every reader has a pet/recipe/life story or whatever is relevant (and a good deal that isn't) and you should be ready for the feedback from readers. This can be one of the most rewarding aspects of column-running if you don't let it take up too much of your writing time. And what else? At the end of every month you are guaranteed a pre-negotiated regular fee without having to invoice anyone.

Reviewing

The very special task of reviewing books, drama, films, videos, radio and television programmes is not work for a newcomer to writing. Reviewing is a highly specialised art.

Book reviewing, for example, is by no means as easy as it might seem. Don't imagine that all you have to do is to read a book you like and write about it. Get this job and you will find that the editor, not you, makes the decision about what you will read. Maybe when you climb the ladder and *run* the book review column or page you will be in a position to make your own choices. Whatever your status in this field, you'll learn to read books not merely as a leisure reader but as a professional reviewer. Balancing the technique of reading in this light with the demands of the paper regarding style, space and deadlines can be very demanding. Most importantly, the specialised art of writing such reviews may turn out to be not the pleasant, easy-going job you envisaged but a hard taskmaster or (dare I mention it?) even tedious. Reviewers are usually allowed a week or ten days to read books and write reviews which must be interesting and lively without being patronising.

Newspapers will often hire someone famous in another sphere to review a book a week – a politician or a top sportsman, say – to attract readers with the name of the reviewer rather than with his ability to review books. However, the quality papers have their own trained and experienced staff reviewers. How, then, do you gain experience? For all categories of reviewing it is only at the discretion of the editor (or features editor, for reviews usually come under his aegis) that you may be given a chance. If you've read this far you will know the only way to build up a solid reputation is to keep writing the copy he wants when (or preferably just before) he wants it; in other words, by demonstrating your professionalism.

An editor is also wary of offering a reviewing job to an unknown for fear of upsetting his staff who may be well qualified to do it. Think too of the author, the playwright, the radio writer or the television scriptwriter who finds his work inadequately covered. A bad review by a professional reviewer is fair enough: a poorly written one by someone who doesn't know what he's doing is not. On one theatre-review job I found myself sitting next to a young man (covering for another paper) who innocently confided to me that he had never before set foot in a theatre. Pity the playwright, the producer, the cast and everyone else – and the newspaper. Most of all, perhaps, pity the young man.

In the quality papers the arts, business, entertainment, sport, finance, women's affairs, employment and leisure pages are major attractions. Although most of the material for these pages is provided by staff writers there is always room for a good freelance who has done a properly researched and well-written job. Geraniums, opera, bridge, tapestry: are these your special subjects? They and many others have provided a first success for freelances who thought they'd never find a way in.

Fillers, letters and small pieces

The quality papers take a serious view of the news, supporting it with informed analysis and comment on political, economic, social and world events – news and comment being kept firmly apart. Letters-to-the-editor are always welcomed but not always printed. If this is your way in (and it is not to be sneered at; many writers have pushed a toe in the door this way), market study will as always dictate your path. How do published letters from readers deal with issues of the day or topics recently covered in earlier issues? To what degree are letters light-hearted or serious? Do they find answers from the paper itself or from other readers? How frequently is your targeted paper open to introducing a letter on a subject not previously (or recently) covered? Of course the length and style of all letters and small items will also be your guide.

Letters to the local press are useful. Scan your local papers for whatever is a new topic rising in importance but don't come in at the end of a discussion or even in the middle; the secret is either to start a new topic of correspondence or to join near the start of its short life. In starting a new topic on the letters page, you will, of course, be mindful of your weightier copy almost ready to send to the editor, on what is then a relevant matter. Make your own peg on which to hang your copy.

The old so-called 'fillers' of yesteryear were popular with freelances who found submitting small pieces quite profitable. Editors used them to fill odd spaces left at the foot of columns or pages where the larger copy had not taken up the space it was intended to cover. Computer typesetting has changed all that and layout is easier to estimate correctly – meaning there are no odd spaces waiting to be filled. Now it is more likely that small pieces will have a little column to themselves – and here will be all sorts of very short pieces, each hardly more than a sentence or two. Newspapermen used to call such columns NIBS (news in brief bits) and on some papers this term is still used, even though the NIBS are not necessarily items of news.

More . . .

Newspapers are printed in ink that quickly makes your fingers dirty. Magazines are on thicker, glossier paper and have their pages stapled, sewn or glued together. So what are the colour supplements which have no existence separate from their big national parents? And what about all the papers/magazines devoted to readers of specialist trades or religious groups, material published by companies for their employees or hobbyist papers for their enthusiasts? Many of these are printed on newsprint but are they newspapers? Since parts of this book are applicable to magazines as well as to newspapers it would seem churlish and short-sighted to leave them on the copy-taster's spike. These supplements are usually the 'specialist' areas of the paper devoted to their particular topics in greater depth than could be accommodated in the pages of their parent papers. This being so, they are harder to break into and demand deeper market study. So watch the supplements carefully. Success here will not be easy but it will work wonders for your confidence as well as adding a big feather to your portfolio to show to other editors.

Is your journalist's mind sufficiently enquiring to want to know how the shopper coped with her skirt caught in a car door in a public car park? She climbed out of it, draped her coat round her legs and walked to the nearest shop selling skirts. From there she rang a garage who came and freed her skirt from the car door. But what if she couldn't get out of the skirt, hadn't got anything to drape round her, couldn't find a shop selling skirts, or anyone to open the car door?

Maybe you ought to be writing fiction . . .

5. Style

What *is* style? I see it as speaking to readers in their own language, appealing to their senses and controlling their reactions. Note that word 'controlling', for this is what we are doing (or trying to do) with everything we write. Such is the power of words. When something can be read without effort you can be sure that effort has gone into its writing – often over hours uncounted and unwitnessed.

Style encapsulates the 'when', 'where' and 'how' to use the English language's strongest words and phrases, skilfully arranged and grouped together for maximum effect. Words to arouse and rivet the attention; phrases to enlighten and appeal to the senses; sentences and paragraphs to bring vision to the eye and understanding to the brain. Style gives words life, and the best style does it without the reader even being aware of its existence.

Some freelances at the start of their careers suspect that well-published experienced writers don't have to concern themselves with style. These lucky folk, they imagine, don't think about style; it just comes naturally to them, flowing down their fingers every time they write. Undoubtedly most readers are blissfully unaware of the work involved in getting words into publishable shape on paper: I have no first-hand understanding of the work going on behind the scenes in, say, designing a block of flats, or organising a ceremonial procession. But truly gifted writers who can write beautifully without any apparent effort? Genius is not unknown but it is very rare indeed. 'It's a funny thing,' commented an elderly writer when asked how he was so successful with everything he wrote. 'The more I read and understand and the harder I work, the more successful I become.'

Ask any group of writers what 'style' is and you may hear a variety of explanations. I do know that thought must be structured before writing can be, and that there is a deal of nonsense written and spoken about style. 'Good taste' is equally vague and entirely subjective. Certainly that which appears to me to be in good taste may not appeal to you at all, so what is one person's style may be another's poison.

Some writers claim that attempting to dissect style is to kill it. I don't agree. People who know me well tell me they can 'hear' my voice in some of what I write (though I'm not sure whether this constitutes praise or criticism) and it is true that your personal style is 'you' as much as your voice, your mannerisms and the way you walk; it cannot be otherwise. To sell successfully to different markets you will need to write in varying styles to satisfy editors who know what kind of writing their particular readers expect, enjoy – and *buy*. Experience will also enable you to write in the required style while still keeping your own voice.

But there is more to it than that. In the following pages I've narrowed down what I think 'style' means. With everything I write my hope is that these factors loiter in the subconscious and weave some sort of spell. Occasionally they do; often they won't.

Clarity

Clarity begins at home. If we don't make what we say crystal clear, we might as well not bother to write it down. Using words readers cannot understand or writing long, meandering sentences that lose their way is a waste of time both for you and for your editors. Everything must be plain, unambiguous and relevant without excessive jargon. Sound grammatical construction and use of positive words in the active voice are among the hallmarks of good writing.

The natives looked friendly but they didn't offer them any food. Who didn't offer any food and who didn't get any? *The natives looked friendly but didn't offer the travellers any food* or *The natives looked friendly but the travellers didn't offer them any food* makes it plain who went hungry.

Girls are now smoking more cigarettes than boys. Do girls really smoke boys?

It is so easy, fatally easy, to assume that readers will understand what we writers don't even recognise as possible causes of misunderstanding.

Accuracy

Being accurate means getting the facts right – and it is important to do so if you don't want the wrath of readers (and therefore of editors) to descend upon your head. You must not only avoid making mistakes about purely *factual* matters, but also ensure that you are using the right words in the right places. *Borrow* and *lend* may be no problem but are you happy about *infer* and *imply*, or *principle* and *principal*, *agoraphobia* and *acrophobia*? What determines whether you use *after* or *afterwards*? I think it downright sneaky, by the way, for *invalid* to be the opposite of *valid* when *invaluable* is not the opposite of *valuable*. And what about *fewer* and *less*? (If you're wondering, *fewer* can be counted but *less* can't.)

Do you find yourself writing phrases like 'expeditiously effected an exit' (left quickly)? Do you write redundant words: 'she filled up the kettle', or 'there was more to follow later'? Are you guilty of 'different to' or 'fed up of"? Accuracy demands we think more carefully about everything we write. One newspaper reported: 'At the age of three her father took her to Canada.' Advanced, wasn't he, for a three-year-old? Although carelessness causes us to write badly we recognise many of our mistakes only when they are brought to our attention by someone else. It's never easy to spot our own.

Grammar

Following the current trend in talking is not necessarily the best way to write for any newspaper. Poor grammar and an apparent ignorance of syntax are common in everyday conversation. You may argue that speech has a brief life, and we don't want to talk like textbooks on English grammar – so it doesn't matter if the rules are broken as long as we know what people mean . . . Ay, there's the rub. Very often the 'rules' are broken to such an extent that we can only guess at what people are trying to say. Yesterday I heard someone talking about a toll bridge newly opened to give access to an island. Local people and tourists are annoyed. Attempting to justify the charges a council official explained: 'You can buy a book of five tickets cheaper than single tickets.' That would be a good bargain if he meant what he said. I could buy a book of tickets and be able to cross five times, for less than the cost of a single ticket allowing me to cross just once. Of course we know he should have said that buying a book of five tickets worked out as less costly than buying five separate tickets. We had to put our own wits to his ill-chosen words in order to make sense of them. But put any solecism, however minor, in writing and you bestow on it a credibility it doesn't deserve. Fortunate will be our council official if, having committed such nonsense to by-law, people don't come along and take him at his word, demanding books of tickets for less than the cost of single ones. Good luck to the people wanting access to the island.

The same poor official fell into another grammatical trap, which you may have identified. He used the word *cheaper* where he should have said *more cheaply*. Adverbs are breeding-grounds for loose writing. Used with discretion they can greatly enhance your copy; that's what they're for, after all. 'Incredibly, inordinately, devastatingly, immortally, calamitously, hearteningly, adorably beautiful.' These were the words of Rupert Brooke in a 1913 (*circa*) letter to Cathleen Nesbitt, the actress, replying to criticism that he was 'in love with words'. Like all words, adverbs are most effective in the right place – and can confuse in the wrong one. *She ate and talked quickly*. Did she eat quickly, talk quickly or do both quickly? Regardless of the answer, *quickly* is an adverb, a word added to a verb to modify it. Many readers won't notice if you use adjectives where you should be using adverbs, but many others will, and it will annoy them – not an encouragement to buy the newspaper again. Alas, you hear it frequently – for example, *the man walked slower than the boy did* instead of *the man walked more slowly than the boy did*. *Slower* is an adjective describing a noun: *he ran a slower race than he had run last week*. While hearing it in casual speech may be a small irritation quickly passed, in print it can be of greater annoyance.

Even the once mighty *Sunday Times* is not above such errors. On 7 July 2002 a front-page item suggested that a particular food-poisoning bug carried by dogs may well be infecting owners and other people. It read *The bacteria occurs in a wide range of strains and mutates so fast* (ugh, ugh – 'fast' is an adjective so this should be 'quickly') *that it has been impossible to find a vaccine against it.*

Here are three adverbial nasties eager to leap in when your back is turned. 'Hopefully' may alter the interpretation of a sentence without the speaker being aware of it. 'It will rain tomorrow' is a bald statement; 'Hopefully it will rain tomorrow' immediately reveals a personal view. People in tents or on beaches might not agree; 'regrettably' could reflect their feelings more accurately. But is rain capable of hope or regret? 'Arguably' is another to argue about – but then, arguably, almost everything is arguable. If 'arguably' is used to give the notion that the writer is behaving fairly, letting readers see both or differing sides of some point of discussion, let the writer find a better way of indicating such open-mindedness. Last of the terrible trio is 'basically'. 'I am thinking (and writing) with reason and knowledge, after clear consideration, and have come to the following simple conclusion to this complex matter which I will now explain to you in terms that you [simpleton] can understand . . .' is what the writer is saying in this weakest of all adverbs. Too often he hasn't considered the 'complex matter' at all. Used carelessly, 'basically', often egged on by its friends 'actually' and 'really' means 'This word sounds intelligent while I try to think of a valid point to forward the discussion.'

Adverbs can enhance your writing, but used clumsily they can ruin it. *The leaf fluttered gently* – how else does anything flutter? *He slammed the door noisily* – can you slam it quietly?

Adjectives

Newspapers use adjectives only when they have a definite purpose on the page. They should extend nouns rather than prop them up. Avoid using them for their own sake and particularly shun clichéd, meaningless double adjectives such as *full unabridged* story, or *great big* ball. Adjectives should inform or describe but never make the reader stop with a query. *Long* doesn't tell him how long; how short is *short*?

And and

And in the newspaper world it is accepted usage to begin a sentence with the word *and* – despite what you may have been taught at school. Rules of grammar are not made to be followed without intelligent thought so if it feels natural (and sounds natural in your head) to break one, in the right place, do so. But (did your school-teacher also tell you not to begin a sentence with 'but'?) before breaking any make sure you are aware of what the normal rules are.

Difficult relations

Grammar has some difficult relations. There are pairs of words that are not interchangeable although most of us are not sure which to use where. Like these:

> The car that the salesman delivered was green.
> The car which the salesman delivered was green.

Which is correct? Hands up who chose the second? Good. The reasoning behind the distinction is this: *that* defines and *which* informs. This is an over-simplification for the sake of clarity; in truth both sentences would be better without *that* or *which* at all. The point is that in the first sentence, 'that' assumes readers already know the salesman delivered a car and I am simply referring to it again so they will know which particular car I'm talking about. In the second sentence 'which' introduces new information about the car regardless of whether or not readers have already heard about it.

Write *actively* and be positive

Firm definite writing undoubtedly makes readers happy. They feel reassured, content and satisfied both with what they are reading and with the newspaper they are holding. So it is wise to avoid flat, hesitant and vague words. By the same policy, avoid negative writing: use the word *not* with care. *He was usually late* is better than *He was not often on time*, and *They were not given a good room* is wailing compared to *Their room could have been better*. It's the difference between thinking of your private pot of gold as being half full or half empty: between an optimistic or a pessimistic outlook on life. Even if you are unaware of the fact, the words you choose and the way you put them together will influence how readers feel and react. A negative style is disheartening, and editors know that readers won't buy a newspaper they find depressing.

Negative writing has another disagreeable habit often heard in speech. 'He's not going to Paris, I don't think,' we say, when what we mean is 'He's not going to Paris, I (do) think.' In speech it has passed before we've bothered about it (unless you're a purist of grammar) but in print it may make the reader pause – or even turn to something more capably written. Colloquial writing in the right place is acceptable. Double negatives (especially when used without intention) are not. To ensure that 'not' doesn't get its beastly little way, think up a positive alternative when you feel a 'not' coming on and express negatives in positive form: *dishonest* instead of *not honest*, *trivial* instead of *not important* and *ignored* instead of *not listened to*. Yet *not* can be used to strong effect in the right place – in antithesis, for example: *not charity, but simple justice* or *Not that I loved Caesar less, but that l loved Rome more*.

Just as a positive statement is more concise than a negative one, so the active voice is usually more vigorous than the passive; it gives an immediate impact. *Holidays were things they never thought about* is clumsy compared to the direct *they never thought about holidays*. This rule does not, of course, mean that the writer should entirely discard the passive voice, which is frequently convenient and sometimes appropriate. *No stone was left unturned* reads more graphically than *he turned over every stone* because even the least well-read reader will find something familiar turning (*sic*) in his mind about the phrase. In considering whether to use the active or passive voice in whatever you are writing, remember, as always, who will be reading your work – and cut out woolly words. *Hunger made her take the food* is preferable to *the reason she took the food was because she was hungry*.

Keep it simple

Writing superfluous words wastes time and clutters up your mind as well as the page. As a good drawing has no unnecessary lines and an efficient machine no unnecessary parts, so good sentences and paragraphs should contain all that is wanted – and nothing more. This doesn't mean that all sentences must be short or that topics merely skim their surfaces, but that every word *counts*. If you find yourself writing just off the topic or round it or just behind or in front of it, that's waffle and should be cut. All words should *be* the topic. Years ago, with all trainee journalists at the time, I was given the essential facts of a story to be written in 300 words. I did it. Then I was taught how to cut it to 200 words *without omitting anything of importance*. I did that, with some difficulty. The next instruction was to reduce it to 100 words with the same parameter – and this was very tricky. But I learned two important lessons about writing for newspapers. One was how to write to a particular length and the other was how much better the writing was for doing so.

Much of what we *might* write can be simplified:

there is no doubt that is better as *doubtless*
used for cooking purposes (*used for cooking*)
owing to the fact that (*due to*, *since* or *because*)
the fact that I had fallen (*my fall*)

Every time you find yourself writing *the fact that* . . . stop writing, go away and do something else – and when you come back, delete it. Other frequently uninvited guests are *which is*, *who was* and their siblings:

Madrid, which is the capital of Spain (*Madrid, the capital of Spain*)

Elizabeth, who was the daughter of Anne (*Elizabeth, Anne's daughter*)

Alan Bennett, that master of style, realised his aged dustbin had disappeared after a visit from the dustmen. 'Knowing nothing of tautology,' he observed wryly, 'they put the dustbin in the dustbin.'

Order, order!

It is not a good idea to start personal pieces like travel articles with 'I' – before you've had a chance to make what you are going to say and how you are going to say it interesting to readers. In speech, the best place for words or groups of words that we want to emphasise is usually at the end of the sentence. But make the sentence too long in print and the reader will have to look back to recall what we are talking about. Result: the impact will fall flat.

We tend to talk in longer sentences than we use in writing because speaking is so much more rapid. It can be a surprise to count the number of words most newspapers use 'in one breath'. Seven or eight is not abnormal for a sentence in the tabloids, especially in that important opening sentence. The first par or intro of any piece has a particular job: to keep people reading. People don't read papers in the same way as they read fiction. They could be reading newspapers while standing at bus stops or taking a quick coffee break so the story in front of them cannot afford a leisurely beginning. Intros, therefore, must get to the point at once, besides being simple and capable of being instantly absorbed. I find my best ones when I'm not sitting at my desk. Maybe I'm driving or in the bath; being denied the help of a scribbling pad forces me to an intro that is vivid and brief – or I'll forget it before I can write it down. When I do, it often says just what I want it to say.

Sentence length in the tabloids, where space is particularly precious, will be short. The 'fog index' is an old method of assessing a paper's density in terms of words written to fill a given space. This mechanical calculation juggles *average sentence length* with *number of long words* to produce the paper's fog index – set at 11–13 for the average reader and at about 14–16 for those of university-level intelligence. Nowadays such impersonal computations have given way to a more touchy-feely approach; get the feel of the paper's density by reading it and absorbing the favoured length of sentences – always remembering that every paper has its own distinctive voice that needs to be listened to. Short pieces mistakenly subdivided into even smaller patchy scraps will also fail, so make sure every piece of writing is the right length for its appeal on the page: neither a solid slab of prose nor brief bits looking lost.

Normally whatever we are writing about needs subdivision into topics, each of which should be made the subject of a paragraph. This is to let readers know we are moving onto a new development in the subject being covered. There's no rule that says you must contain all you want to say at that moment in a single par; it is more important not to deter a reader with an indigestible block of words. As with sentences, varying the length of paragraphs makes for a lighter and more easily digested article. Variety in paragraph construction is also important in making the written piece easy on the eye and effortlessly taken into the head.

Phrases out of order may be misinterpreted. *She died in Brisbane where she was born in 1951.* Was 1951 the year she was born or the year she died? *She went to America with her mother when she was 30.* Who was 30, mother or daughter? *Specialists in broken furniture* was a thoughtlessly worded newspaper advertisement that made readers laugh. A witness in court said, 'Sitting in the bus the car turned left.' A car was sitting in a bus? And then turned left? The law demands accuracy and the judge was patient. 'Do you mean you were sitting in a bus and saw the car turn to the left?' 'No,' came the bemused reply, 'I was in the car behind.' Further questioning revealed the witness had seen her brother sitting in a bus and he had told her he saw the car turning left.

Folk who don't care about grammar may say 'Why bother? It's the meaning that counts, not the precise words or their order.' In casual speech we can generally understand what is meant even when it is badly expressed. Sometimes we can even do this when we read it in print. But it is still poor writing – and for many people who appreciate good writing, it rankles.

I hope the confusion that sometimes occurs when folk who consider grammar and punctuation to be beneath them is enough to convince wavering readers of its importance. Consider this: '*The boys, who arrived too late, found all the tickets had been sold.*' Both those commas should be omitted. A comma works hard in its role of providing a breathing space for the reader but this sentence is short enough not to need one. Note the difference between a subsidiary clause that *defines* (contributing information of substance) and one that *describes* (merely adding information). Not sure which is which? If it can be left out without hurting the sentence it's descriptive. There are instances where this test doesn't apply but they are rare. Defining clauses hate being fenced off between commas. In the sentence quoted above, 'who arrived too late' is plainly definitive as it explains why they didn't get any tickets. More subtly, sandwiching 'who arrived too late' between commas bestows on it less significance than what you imply is to follow. As that is not the case here the reader is left with a whiff of dissatisfaction.

Changing the sentence to '*The boys, who were wearing green shirts, found* . . .' makes the subsidiary clause descriptive; it adds information by telling us the colour of the boys' shirts. Apply the test. The commas should be left in place. You disagree? Cut them out, then, and we're left with '*The boys who were wearing green shirts found all the tickets had been sold.*' Ah, readers not party to this discussion might think, so boys in red or yellow or blue shirts got tickets but the organisers refused to sell any to green shirt-wearers. No, that's not what we mean, is it? There must be something in this punctuation business after all; it's not just pedantic nonsense. 'The writer who neglects punctuation, or mispunctuates, is liable to be misunderstood,' wrote Edgar Allan Poe. 'For the want of merely a comma, it often occurs that an axiom appears a paradox, or that a sarcasm is converted into a sermonoid.' (That's an unusual word to send us scurrying to our dictionaries.)

Alas, writing good English and punctuating it well is one thing but writing for newspapers can be rather different. Only you can decide which markets to write for and the work you do. Should you ever feel disheartened about standards remember there are papers to satisfy everybody. No matter which you choose you must put yourself in the place of their readers if you wish to sell.

Old hat or cool?

In appreciating the importance of keeping abreast of modern thought and idiom, how are your clichés? Phrases and sayings are sharp and appropriate the first time round, not so endearing when you've heard them a few times and a bore when you find them at every turn. So today's clichés may be tomorrow's groans. There's nothing new under the sun? A touch of satire, perhaps, or a whiff of teasing may lighten copy of a serious nature if used in the right place. Clichés thoughtlessly used are to be avoided like the plague (*sic*) but they make a handy tool in skilled hands. So don't eschew them just because they are so frequently misused. They exist to be used, but wisely. Stereotyped writing is another hazard. Do you use phrases that should have lain down and died years ago? (Is 'lain' the right word here or do you suspect it should be 'laid'?)

Never forget we are writing for newspapers, most of which have a very short life. Using words and phrases in current fashion may keep us on the up-to-date level of many of our readers – as long as we don't overdo it. Although 'twenty-four seven', for instance, might be normal parlance for many readers, others will need an explanation that it is idiomatic for 'twenty-four hours a day, seven days a week'. No editor will insert such explanation so the term will simply baffle those who don't know what it means. What the editor is more likely to do, however, is not to accept copy that uses idioms he fears his readers will not understand. Market study is poking its head up again.

If market study deems it appropriate (and it frequently does) don't be afraid of writing with emotion in moderation. Words on paper have no inflections or nuances in themselves. A well-established lesson much feared by trainees teaches this quite ruthlessly; their written work is read aloud to them in relentless monotone, with no attempt at voice inflection or word/phrase interpretation. Ask someone to try it with your words. It is a sobering experience which starkly reminds us that words are all we writers can put in cold print on a newspaper page; just words – so we'd better make them arouse the senses and visual images to touch and release emotion in our readers. At the same time beware of letting your imagination be overblown into 'purple prose' which will only interfere with the story. *Desperation plucked at her throat* is not for newspaper pages. Underplay, rather than overplay, to evoke emotion. We are writing for real people and only our perception and skill in painting wordpictures will attract them.

On the house

All newspapers have what they call a 'house style', which is very different from the style we've been talking about. House style is just a particular way of doing things, of how the pages are set up, what typefaces are used: defined ways of laying things out. The idea is to try and present a uniformity to a variety of different journalists' work and most papers seem to achieve this remarkably successfully. You will have to conform to this house style if you are to get your work accepted. Getting a 'feel' for it will only come from regular reading of the newspaper. Note how dates are printed. Tuesday, 23rd August, 2005 may be perfectly correct, but the local regional may insist on Tuesday 23 August 2005. (For the fastidious: check your calendars.)

Observing the house style means following established rules and customs in punctuation, paragraphing, the use of capital letters and hyphens, the precise way of writing numbers, dates, abbreviations and everything else that has to be set in text. As your copy will be set in columns, spare the dashes; they can make newspaper columns look gappy and unkempt. William Rees-Mogg, when editor of *The Times*, put in the style book a prohibition on any sentence more than 12 words long. Whatever the house rules are they exist only for the convenience of everyone writing for the paper (no more uncertainty about whether to give them '1,2,3' or 'one, two, three' and so on) and for consistency. It would look ill-organised to print 'Doctor Jack Harris' in one par and refer to him lower down the page as 'Dr. J. Harris', or to print 'etcetera' on page 2 and 'etc' on page 4. The latter raises a typical house style problem: 'etcetera' is, I think, unique in being spoken in full but commonly written in abbreviated form. In its shortened form does 'etc' have a full stop after it when it's in the middle of a sentence, only at the end of a sentence, in both situations or in neither?

How do you refer to the house where the Jones family lives? *The Jones' house*, *The Jones's house* or *The Joneses's house*? The house style will supply the answer. But now comes the bad news: many newspapers do not have a written copy of their house-style book to give you or even show you. Often they are rules unwritten but known by custom and practice to everyone working and writing for the paper. If you can't get hold of a house-style book (and a request for one may be treated with bemused astonishment) I suggest you make your own by keeping an eye on the newspaper of your choice and making a note of any quirkiness that may trip you up.

Scaffolding and construction

If the reader has to adjust his interpretation of what he's reading half-way through your copy (and go back and start again if he's sufficiently interested) there's something seriously wrong with it. Capricious scaffolding could be the weakness. Only the designer knows it was there, it was the only structure that held the whole edifice together at the beginning and nothing could have been built at all without it. A writer is the designer and the builder but first he has to erect the scaffolding – and make sure it is strong.

Newspaper writing is quite unlike fiction where the crunch will be saved to the end. Newspaper readers don't want to wade through a long story, even one full of enticing leads and hints, to find out how it ends. For us the conclusion comes first and the rest of the story comes next, in order of importance. Think of your structure as a pyramid; the most important facts comes in the first (lead) sentence or at the latest in the opening paragraph, to draw readers into the story and make them want to read on. Next comes the rest of the story in descending order of importance. Apart from pulling readers into the story, this form of structure allows any editor or sub-editor to cut copy from the bottom of the pyramid, if he has to, without losing the most important part of the story.

Balancing this pyramid structure is the need not to end with a weak whimper – and therein lies the skill in just one of the aspects of writing with 'style' (*see* also page 56).

Another helpful tip for any kind of writing is to speak what you have written out loud. The involuntary repetition of a particular 'shape' can make one paragraph look like another regardless of its content. Read a couple of pages of a feature in a quality daily or regional paper and notice how adopting a different strategy for each par avoids giving readers the same doorstep to climb over and over again. If you find it hard to identify different paragraph shapes, listen to the radio and imagine you have to present in written form a report about, say, Peruvian rug-making. As you listen, think where you would end one paragraph and open a new one.

The topic and slant will determine the tenor of the pars you write, so that a news story, for example, will be written more crisply than a feature. Whatever it is, does narration tell the story effectively or is exposition more appropriate? Just telling your reader what happened may be rather flat; exposition, *showing* what happened, is more effective. Remember being told something by a friend who put actions, voice, body and facial expression into the story? What makes you remember it is the way he told it to you. Join a group when one person is trying to tell the others something. 'Go on,' he might say to another in the group, 'you tell them'. He knows that the second speaker will, probably without being aware of what he is doing, use exposition rather than mere narration. This exposition is also instinctive to published writers albeit they have only the printed page on which to place their words. With style, you can see the gestures and hear the voices *in your mind's eye* – and so can your readers. And every paragraph, every sentence and even every word, is keeping the story moving. Being specific is better than being general and plain words are often best. Write as readers talk but don't copy casual talk without thinking. Sloppy writing like *at this moment in time* or *at the end of the day* is not likely to endear you to any editor. And here's another tip.

To build the written piece, one paragraph has to follow its predecessor smoothly; it needs a 'joiner'. Two sentences before this one you've had one of the best. A newspaper writer knows he must keep readers reading and that means keeping them sufficiently interested to bridge the mental jump of eye and brain from one paragraph to the next. That's hardly a difficult jump, you might be thinking – but drifting to another item on the page is sometimes easier. So we use a technique to keep people reading by leaving a little 'come-on' dangling at the end of a paragraph. Go back to the last paragraph which ends with a short sentence, 'And here's another tip.' This is a 'come-on' to entice you into reading the following one – although this device is less appropriate in books and I use it here merely to illustrate a technique. A good public speaker will use the same procedure before pausing to take a sip of water, to deter folk in the audience from using the break to make a rush for the exit.

Paragraph joiners may be phrases or single words and you can spot them at the start of many a good par. Out of place, they can make your paragraphs overdressed; *moreover*, *nevertheless* and *notwithstanding* make the less portentous *however* more acceptable but even that is hardly the normal parlance of tabloid readers. *All the same* and *even so* are more comfortable, but – as always – the market is king. *Yet*, *but*, *despite* and conjunctions of time like *when* come naturally. Many joiners serve more than the purpose of linking one paragraph to the previous one. Just as *and* continues with what you're saying, *for* introduces a reason, a result, or a new development, so is tantamount to saying *and the consequence is*, *or was* and *but* involves a stepping back and looking at the matter from the other side. *Now* can be patronising and should be used with care. It may be a complacent pause by a writer more fascinated by what he's writing than is good for him; usually what it says is *at last we're getting to the point of this story*.

It must be the ease with which punctuation is sprinkled about that makes it so tempting but it is best used with restraint. Its *raison-d'être* is two-fold: to facilitate smooth reading and to ensure that what has been written is not misunderstood. In its latter capacity it guards against ambiguity – but if you don't know your colon from your inverted commas your punctuation could be doing quite the reverse. We need to know the function of the different punctuation marks and where they should be placed. All emphasis is no emphasis and to overdo punctuation is a mistake. Remember that fashions come and go even in punctuation. At one time the accepted format for 'one, two and three' was to insert a comma before 'and'. Now that extra comma (known as the 'Oxford' comma from its popularity with the Oxford University Press) is usually discarded. But there is still a need for it at times; consider 'shopping in Marks and Spencers and Woolworths'. Anyone familiar with shopping would almost certainly know how many shops were visited; a stranger, if asked, might reply, 'Three.' Be particularly careful in the use of exclamation marks which are usually unnecessary and undesirable. British novelist and literary critic E M Forster considered them the equivalent of laughing at your own jokes and he was right. Too often they mean *see how clever I am!!!*

Are you in need of a brush-up on what you learned at school or can't remember learning? Can you identify a *synonym*? ('A synonym is a word you use when you can't spell the word you first thought of,' according to American composer Burt Bacharach.) Do you know when to use *shall* or *will*? Can you tell a transitive verb from an intransitive one? Do you know what a *collective noun* is? Or a *relative pronoun*? Take a few hours a week (or even a few minutes a day) to browse through the *Guide to English in the 21st Century* by Godfrey Howard, one of the best of its kind.

Professional journalists use countless tricks of the trade every day: implying something without actually saying it, repetition for a particular reason, slowing up or quickening pace, deliberate facetiousness, compression and emphasis for a special effect. All these techniques give impact and colour. Read papers with a new eye and you can't help but learn more. And when your copy is published always compare it with what you put in, and learn from the difference.

He and she & his and hers

The problem of 'he or she', 'him or her', and associated uncertainties is a constant thorn in newspaper copy. 'I like Cheddar cheese. But everyone to his or her favourite.' Does anybody like the taste of that artificial if grammatically correct slab of cheese? Let's try grilling it. The sentence may be recast in several ways – perhaps 'people have their favourites' or 'everyone has a favourite'. 'We all have our favourites' is a third solution and the one I would choose, partly because it flows more easily in print but chiefly because the 'we' puts me on the same level as the readers and everything I write should be viewed through their eyes. Using the first person plural gives this 'one of us' feeling quite naturally. Contrast such usage with 'It is thought' or 'It is said' (by whom, anyway?) which is totally impersonal. In quality papers in the right circumstances, fine; in lighter vein it digs a ditch between you and your readers, who may not bother to jump over it.

He said, she said, etc. – and when?

In reporting direct speech it is tempting to rely on 'he/she said', 'the speaker added' and similar phrases. To avoid tedious repetition it is important to find other ways of leaving the reader in no doubt about which words you are attributing to which speaker. A variety of words meaning 'said' will not do. You will soon run out of 'laughed', 'grumbled', 'shouted' and 'whispered' and readers will start looking for your next verbal gyration and stop listening to the story you are telling. Often it will be clear from the context just who is speaking. Punctuation and layout on the page will help but be cautious about writing *today*, *tomorrow*, *last year* and any words or phrases relating to time. These terms will be meaningless (and confusing) when your work is published and should always be more clearly defined: *March 2004, in early summer*, etc.

Euphony

Euphony is a funny thing. You only notice it when it isn't there. Written work, be it a news story, an article, a brief piece or just a Letter to the Editor, may be silent words on paper, but take them all together and there is – or should be – a rhythm, a satisfaction, a *something* that helps the reader feel at the end, 'Yes, that was well written.' You think this is inflated talk that would be scorned by your local paper or freesheet? Not at all. As children learning to read we hear the words in our heads and at an early age we say them aloud. With maturity comes that curious state of absorbing what we read without being aware of it; we no longer read individual words strung together but whole pieces of written work.

A parallel state exists when we writers refer to the 'flow of writing' or 'being in full flow' and perhaps when that is happening the euphony factor is taking over subconsciously exactly as we want it to. It's easy to spoil it, to 'lose the flow', as we all know. A muddled phrase, getting facts wrong, chasing up a blind alley and then trying to write our way out of trouble – all these can break the euphony. So can a sudden unwarranted switch in viewpoint or tense, a misplaced adverb or inconsistency in mood. In practical terms inadequate attention to structure, paragraph size and punctuation can jar readers out of sympathy in a trice. When that happens they immediately lose their absorption capacity. Euphony gives way to exasperation. They may start reading the paragraph or sentence again with jaded interest all too easily abandoned, or they may not bother at all.

Don't hang about

When your piece is done, how do you end it? This is called 'casting-off'. Its prime demand is urgency; when you've finished, *finish*. If you meander on with extra thoughts you should have inserted earlier or ones that don't belong in the story a sub-editor will cast-off for you. Then it may not be a cast-off so much as a cut-off which is usually as unsatisfactory an experience as is its verbal cousin on the telephone. Casting-off simply means ending the story succinctly and at the right time. Cutting-off is what the sub-editor does when the copy overruns. It is either too long for the space allotted for it or, more probably, it doesn't end at the end of the story. Woe to the writer whose work is cut-off. If you have saved your *pièce de résistance* till the end it's likely to suffer a *coup de grâce*.

The clues are there to follow . . .

As with every other aspect of writing for newspapers, the paper itself provides all the clues. If it could speak it would say what editors themselves want writers to know about style: professionally written copy, 'tight' writing, irresistible openings and an imaginative fresh approach. For popular newspapers adopt a relaxed conversational style backed by solid research and clearly presented as if you're talking to a friend. Observing the rules of basic grammar is no more than acquiring the ability to write good English.

Careful market study reveals that a single newspaper may adopt different styles on different pages. News reporting, for example, will generally be straightforward and factual wherever it appears. Features can tell a different story; the tabloids, tighter on space, favour concise copy but up-market titles also want crispness *in their own way*. For all markets the choice of words and their arrangement in sentences and paragraphs must be made to capture the heads and hearts of readers. *Care* about your story. If you don't, why should they? Some writers say, 'I can't get my style right.' This is nonsense. Let it grow in your mind and develop its own personality. Your style may be you, or it may be you instinctively absorbing the style of your target newspaper. Let it mature and it will serve you well.

The same can be said about any reputable English dictionary – and there are several. It is always wise to consult more than one for they may vary in their definitions and contents. Among my favourites are:

- The big multi-volume *Oxford English Dictionary* (OED) and the *Shorter Oxford English Dictionary* (SOED). The OED is the accepted authority on the evolution of the English language over the last millennium. It is an unsurpassed guide to the meaning, history and pronunciation of over half a million words, both present and past. It traces the usage of words through 2.5 million quotations from a wide range of international English language sources, from classic literature and specialist periodicals to film scripts and cookery books. It covers words from across the English-speaking world, from North America to South Africa, from Australia and New Zealand to the Caribbean. It also offers the best in etymological analysis, listings of variant spellings, and shows pronunciation using the international phonetic alphabet. The Second Edition of the OED is currently available as a 20-volume print edition, on CD-ROM, and now also online.
- The single-volume dictionaries by Chambers and Collins.
- *The New Fowler's Modern English Usage* (often just called Fowler's).
- *Waterhouse on Newspaper Style* (Viking, 1989) and *English our English* (Viking, 1991) by Keith Waterhouse (old but unbeatable when you want more than just the correct way to write brilliant English).
- *The Penguin Dictionary of Troublesome Words* by Bill Bryson (whose suggested alternative title is *A Guide to Everything in English Usage That the Author Wasn't Entirely Clear About Until Quite Recently*).

- *website* http://www.dictionary.com/doctor (free online English dictionary and reference guide which also answers questions about words, grammar and language).

English is now widely spoken on six continents. It is the primary language of the United Kingdom, the United States, Canada, Australia, Ireland, New Zealand, and various small island nations in the Caribbean Sea and the Pacific Ocean. It is also an official language of India, the Philippines, and many countries in sub-Saharan Africa, including South Africa. English is also closely related to Frisian, German, and Netherlandic (Dutch and Flemish).

In the 16th century it was the mother-tongue of only a few million people living in England, but colonisation spread it across the globe until by the late 20th century more than 350 million people claimed it as their native language. Today it is the mother tongue of more people than any other language except Mandarin Chinese. English is the most widely taught foreign language and the most widely used second language – i.e. one used for mutual communication when people cannot understand each other's first tongue. Throughout the world one person in seven speaks English as either a primary or a secondary language.

The words of the English language can be divided according to their function or form into roughly eight parts of speech: nouns, pronouns, adjectives, verbs, adverbs, prepositions, conjunctions and interjections. In English syntax, the main device for indicating the relationship between words is word order. For example, in the sentence *The girl loves the boy* the subject is in initial position, and the object follows the verb; transposing the order of *boy* and *girl* would change the meaning. Other languages do not always follow this pattern and memories of schoolday Latin classes, for instance, may remind you that the words themselves are inflected, i.e. changed, to indicate their grammatical significance. *Puerum puella amat* is the Latin equivalent of *The girl loves the boy*, and even when the words are given in a different order (*Amat puella puerum*) the meaning remains the same.

Linguistic experts tell us it is the lack of such precision that makes English a very easy language to speak or write *poorly*.

And that is why we writers must take extra care in how we use our only tool – words. We have the largest vocabulary of any language in the world, but browsing through any dictionary soon reveals how little most of us value it and what a tiny proportion of its treasures we ever use at all.

Those who decry what they consider too much attention to 'style' and spelling are quick to point out that compilers of dictionaries have always had their critics. In 1746 Samuel Johnson wrote *The Plan of a Dictionary of the English Language*, not the first dictionary to be published but the most successful. It was published in weekly parts at sixpence each so it must have reached a wide audience. (As a matter of interest to freelance writers in any century, Johnson claimed that the best biographies were written by those who had eaten and drunk and 'lived in social intercourse' with their subjects.)

Spelling has always been an object of scepticism. When Noah Webster published his first *American Dictionary* more than 50 years after Johnson, it was greeted with much derision (regarding spelling) on this side of the Atlantic – and to this day we accept Anglo-American differences with amused tolerance. Use of the internet has revitalised the apparently endless debate about whether spelling matters or not. 'Freespelling', a campaign to reform (in its true meaning of re-form) the spelling of words like *yacht* (yot?) and *fuchsia* (fewsher?), met with apt words from columnist Philip Howard in the pages of *The Times*. 'Our spelling does gradually change to reflect new styles and pronunciations,' he said. 'It is changing in the great pond of the internet and the little puddles of text msging. But free-for-all spelling would deface and barbarise the English tongue. It would empty it of the hoarded wit, wisdom, poetry and history which it contains. And it ain't going to happen.'

'Those who prefer their English sloppy have only themselves to thank if the advertisement writer uses his mastery of vocabulary and syntax to mislead their weak minds.' Dorothy L Sayers

6. Rewriting

Rewrite and rewrite until you are sure your work is as appealing to your readers as it can be. When it is and you see it in print, you'll realise that the rewards are far greater than the trouble you took – and it will all have been worth it. A piece I wrote recently about bathroom suites carried the phrase 'the ultimate in convenience' – or that's what I *intended* it to do. Only on reading it through did I notice I had described an expensive piece of the latest bathroom equipment as '*the ultimate inconvenience*'. Only a tiny fault in not hitting the space bar at the right moment, but . . .

Some writers expect editors to tell them what is wrong with their copy and how to put it right. Although this is not an editor's job (and he wouldn't have time to do it even if he wanted to) when he receives freelance copy that is so brilliant he *must* have it, he will probably clean it up or let his staff do so. He will consider whether the value of the piece is worth the effort involved in licking it into shape – perhaps it needs little more than the correcting of a few literals (typing errors, generally). On the whole we must work on the principle that the finished product we submit to an editor must speak for itself. It must do so in several respects and it is important to check them all.

- The content and style adhere to the expected (or promised) pattern (i.e. stick to the point).
- You plunge straight into the story – are you sure you haven't started with some waffle that does not relate to the central point? The task of encouraging readers to read further falls firmly on this opening sentence, or even the first words of it.

- There is no clutter. If you have done a lot of research for your work you may be tempted to use every last scrap of it. Don't. Some may not be strictly relevant to what you are writing now but should be kept aside, perhaps for a later piece for a different editor. No research is ever wasted but the use of it to best effect requires discipline, all the more so if what you long to include in your copy (but know isn't relevant) is something you find particularly fascinating. Research is a good tool but a poor master. If you want to make use of some interesting facts or figures but fear they are cluttering up the text, pull them out and put them in a sidebar.
- Your copy must be impeccably dressed. This means flawlessly typed or printed on clean A4 paper no less than 70 grams in weight and always white. Flawlessly means just that: no mistyped or misplaced punctuation marks, no hand-written crossing out or insertion, and every page correctly numbered. Word-processing laughs at small errors as it is so simple to correct them.

You may consider this pedantic nonsense but reflect on the impression that badly presented copy gives an editor when he first sees it. He's bound to wonder whether the writer is equally careless in whatever research lies behind the copy. Can he rely on given telephone numbers or the spelling of names? Hmm. He can't be sure. And when an editor isn't sure he won't take a risk. Why should he? There is other copy waiting to be read – from other more fastidious freelances.

When you are rewriting or making corrections, be careful you don't make more mistakes in doing so. 'Cut and paste' is a little miracle-worker but omitting to tidy up your copy when you think you've finished can result in a mess. What was a full stop ending a sentence may still be there after you've pasted another bit onto it – so go through your amended version with a toothcomb. It's easy to miss half-sentences or duplicated paragraphs or printed gobbledegook resulting from careless corrections. I don't wholly trust spell-checkers. I understand they can't (or won't) put me right with *there*, *their* and *they're*, for instance, and they won't stop me writing *not* when I mean to write *now*, both being correctly spelt words out of context. But they're not helpful *in* context. What *is* helpful is printing out finished copy for close inspection. No matter how large your on-screen font the eye picks out mistakes more easily on paper in your hand.

Even commissioned work is better received if it is inviting to read; a sub-editor will approach neat copy with more optimism and be less likely to chop it about in sheer irritation. It hardly needs saying that your print should be crisp and clear, so discard worn-out ribbons and replace faint ink cartridges. Luckily for us most modern printers cease printing when there is insufficient ink in cartridges to make a fair impression – a warning it's time to replace the cartridge.

Word processors can be very beguiling, luring you into indulgences with a wide use of fancy typefaces. Resist. Whatever styles the paper of your choice may prefer and however attractive the feature pages may be, wise freelances keep to a plain non-proportional format. And never justify your text; you cannot know exactly how it will appear in print and someone else will have to take time and trouble in *un*justifying it. (Another reason for rejection, perhaps?) Take care with underlining too, for to underline text tells the typesetter to put it in italics, which may not be what you intend at all.

The keys marked 'i', 'l' and '1' are waiting on the keyboard to trap the unwary. Are you typing every uppercase or lowercase 'eye' or 'ell' as you mean it to be? The figure '1' may be a false friend. George 111 was last spotted in the editorial columns of the *Guardian* who should know we have never had a King George the one-hundred-and-eleventh. Neatness means double-spacing on one side of A4 paper, allowing wide margins all round (4 cm and perhaps 4 or 4.5 cm at the top of the first page) with pages numbered, preferably in the top right corner. (A confession here: I always use 1½ line-spacing to save paper – no editor has ever objected.) The first page is generally not numbered. If you run to several pages it is sensible to head them with a single 'catchline', giving an identifying word or phrase at the top of each page beside the page number. The purpose of a catchline is to identify where your page belongs should it be separated from its fellows, and the identifier may be anything you wish. I chose 'hoots', for example, for an article about Florence Nightingale's pet owlet called Athena (but I could equally well have chosen 'Athena'), giving pages the catchline of

'Jill Dick, hoots, page 3 of 6' and 'Jill Dick, hoots, page 4 of 6', etc. Repeating your name on each page (if it is not too long to fit in a single catchline) will also be bringing it to the editor's attention, in your private bit of 'subliminal' advertising – which can't be bad. Any catchline will suffice, but be original to avoid any confusion, and underline your catchline to separate it from the copy itself. Type 'more' or 'mf' at the foot of pages other than the last and finish your copy with the word 'end'.

That's not quite the end because it is helpful to editors to give your wordage. Quote the number of words you have written to the nearest ten if under 100 and in fifties from 100 upwards. So 1,387 would be 1,400 and 1,263 would be 1,250. Don't add 'approx', as if you might be sued for miscounting. Complete your copy with your name, address, phone number (and fax number and email address, if applicable) on the last page below your copy and the wordage.

Start the first paragraph at the left margin but indent the first line of subsequent ones three spaces. Never leave an extra line-space between paragraphs and leave only *one* character space between the end of one sentence and the beginning of the next. Give your copy a heading and if it is a long piece (approaching several hundred words or more) break it up on the page by inserting 'crossheads' (sometimes called 'shoulders') in the text at suitable intervals. This is particularly important as editors thrive on headlines; a rapid skim through crossheads gives them an instant notion of what your copy is all about. It's unlikely that the crossheads will be used as you set them but they will help the copy look more appealing on the pages. You do not know where your copy will appear, nor what may flank it on either side, but ease and speed of reading is what you are aiming for at the submission stage. Give some thought to the heading you choose for your work – although, as with crossheads, it may not be used when your copy appears in print. (Some capriciously printed headlines raise a smile: 'Midshipman dies after drowning at private pool' and 'Judge accused of being impartial' are two of my favourites.) If you have mentioned in your copy that tips or points will be found in an accompanying sidebar, check to make sure it is there and it does contain everything you promised it would.

On the whole, newspapers don't bother with a 'cover sheet' or 'title page' (call it what you will) attached to the front of the copy with details of who you are, what you are writing about and so on. They are more interested in getting to the point – and that (they hope) is to be found in the first paragraph on page one. So I recommend putting whatever you have to say in a brief letter attached to your copy. Like this:

Dear Mr Bloggs,
Further to our conversation on 14 March I enclose a 1,200-word piece about the recent finding of Saxon remains in the old target fields on the west side of Sawlingham.

You will recall I am the official antiquarian at Blowmington Museum and have published several articles on earlier finds in this area in the past ten years.
Yours sincerely,

That's enough to remind editor Bloggs of what you are offering and why you are the best person to write it. Write on your headed paper and remember to date your letter but do not bother with a stamped self-addressed envelope if you have made earlier contact with Mr Bloggs and he is expecting your copy. Computers can easily be set to print two copies of each sheet so keep one of them in your records. There's nothing like a duplicate in your hand for the comfort of seeing what you've submitted. I admit I rely on storage on a computer hard disk alone for short pieces, or for items that I know will be published within a day or two. But this can be dangerous and I do not advise it unless you're prepared to risk losing your copy altogether. Some writers also fear that the inclusion of an SAE is too tempting an invitation for the editor or his secretary to stuff a rejection slip in it and put it in the 'out' tray. Assuming the matter of what rights you are offering has already been agreed, a simple 'first rights' at the foot of your copy will adequately cover this point. Cut off any spare paper on the letter sheet so the fact that your copy starts on the next sheet, without any more preamble, is immediately apparent.

A paper won't object if you want to use a pseudonym but make sure the accounts department knows your real name so you have no problems with paying cheques into your bank.

The best time to send your copy will depend on what arrangements you have already made with the editor (if any), the frequency of publication, your topic and forthcoming seasonal events – among other matters. Christmas editions of papers are always planned well in advance, as much as is possible. Perhaps an editor may be more kindly disposed towards you and the world in general on a Monday than on a jaded Friday, and a quick phone call to his secretary or the telephone switchboard (if there is one) will tell you when he's coming back from his holidays. He may be feeling particularly benevolent toward the first copy he sees on his desk that morning.

Packing and postage

Finally, the packing and postage. For two or three A4 sheets it is enough to fold them over once and use a 23 × 16 cms envelope. For more A4 sheets a larger envelope that will take them without folding is preferable. Life is really too short for second-class stamps so send copy first class if you can. I know it costs a few pence more each time, but if you're in business, you're in business . . .

To keep the ball rolling you could try phoning the editor's secretary a few days after posting to check that your copy arrived. If she knows about it, *resist the temptation to ask any further questions*. Does the editor like it? Is he going to use it, and when? She probably doesn't know the answers and it wouldn't be her place to tell you if she did, unless she were specifically instructed to do so.

Disk checking

Accompanying your hard (printed) copy should be the identical work on disk. Make sure it is in the approved format. Microsoft Word is widely used but check with the editor or his secretary exactly which format to use before making your submission as there are other popular formats. It is important to check, before sending your disk, that it is not corrupted in any way. Run it through a good virus-checker and load your copy directly from it for another check. Have any gremlins wormed their way into your text? Did odd and superfluous characters creep in where you've used formatting commands like underlining or italics? Only careful study of your own copy on disk will put your mind at ease – and not drive the editor out of his.

The balancing act

Undoubtedly rewriting is the key to *good* writing – but where do you stop? Rewrite to excess and you either paralyse what you've written or end up with nothing worthwhile. With the best of intentions you can unwittingly rob copy of its freshness and flatten its impact. Give yourself time and let your work rest (if you can) before looking at it with new eyes: not yours, but your editor's. Learning, by trial and error, is the only way to keep your balance.

'*When I say writing, O, believe me, it is rewriting that I have chiefly in mind.*' Robert Louis Stevenson

7. Interviewing

The essence of a good newspaper is its human interest for that is what it's all about – people. And there can be no closer identification between readers and a person in the public eye than the face-to-face interview. In the hands of a reliable interviewer who knows how to do the job, readers can feel that it was they, not you, who heard your interviewee's voice. They 'saw' him and were fascinated by what he had to say. (And of course if 'he' is female, they saw her as well.)

If we freelances are in the position of being able to choose whom to interview it is not always wise to let our own preferences dictate to us. Many suitable people will not be well known in more than their immediate areas, whereas an achievement of special interest or a personal story from an unknown person could make ideal material. In the first case the attraction will be the interviewee: in the second it will be his story. Either or both could be valid reasons for your choice if you can satisfy yourself about the ultimate question: is the project of sufficient interest to the paper's readers for the editor to accept your idea? From your own point of view, if you are a beginner in the craft of interviewing and nervous about jumping your first hurdle, choosing a less well-known victim could be wise and give you confidence for the future. So how do you find your first interviewee?

Read newspapers, particularly local newspapers, listen to news bulletins, and keep your eyes and ears open wherever you go. Find people at work, on buses or trains, in shops, in clubs or cafés or pubs – anywhere. If they can't be interviewed then and there (or if you're not sufficiently experienced for on-the-spot interviews) talk to them and find their stories. If they 'feel' like good material, fix a date, time and place for an interview with them. It is an enormous help to have already established with an editor that you are going to interview someone for his pages. Then you may use the power of your publication to gain your interviewee's consent. Oh yes, he will think, that's a reliable paper – and both he and you will look forward to the interview with confidence. Most genuine people are modest and profess they are not worthy enough to be interviewed, but with a little persuasion (which is what they probably want) they will yield to your request.

The person whom you interview is most likely to be a celebrity – someone in the news for a particular reason at a particular time. Don't let that word 'celebrity' deter you: a road-sweeper who found a valuable ring in the gutter and returned it to the police station is just as much a celebrity, in interview-worthiness, as someone who has just performed an act of bravery on a cliff face. It is important that they are the only people able to tell a particular story and that it is a story your paper's readers will want to read. Anyone with an unusual story to tell – a sporting champion, the author of a recent best-seller, a leading pop star or someone in the news for any other reason – these are the people readers of newspapers want to know about. Hundreds of people would be thrilled to have the opportunity of talking to their favourite personalities, to sit alone and uninterrupted in a room with plenty of time to ask everything they wanted to know. Think of yourself as the luckiest person in the world to be chosen to do this job and it will soon become a pleasure rather than an ordeal.

It is important to understand the difference between a published interview and a piece merely about a particular person. The latter, sometimes called a 'profile', may concentrate on a single individual but will take a broader view including, perhaps, details and information about the childhood, background and past history of the person being discussed, with the opportunity to write from a more detached standpoint. An interview, albeit it with a similar background of research and investigation, is a one-to-one meeting; its product is a close, personal and *original* result of the meeting and the interviewer's interpretation of it.

Perhaps your potential interviewee is well known and an editor may know more about him than you do, in the early stages. He will certainly know (or can soon find out) if rival papers are planning a similar interview. It's possible your subject may not merit the publicity the paper needs for a particular sales target; there could already be an interview with him in the pipeline; he may have a reputation, unknown to you, of demanding preposterous fees or making impossible conditions and of being more trouble than he is worth. But when all bodes well and the interviewee is just right for the paper, an editor will be even more pleased if he can arrange prior publicity. Circulation, revenue and the paper's image will receive a welcome boost.

Why are you doing the interview?

The best interviewers are not born but made. Above all they are good listeners. Have you the right personality? It takes special perceptiveness and a greater degree of shrewdness and sympathy than many people possess, plus a liberal dose of tact, discretion and the ability to remain silent when required. Being able to rely on your own judgement is also important and (luckily) this confidence in yourself grows with practice. What is more, with experience you'll find that newspaper interviewing becomes fun rather than work. You meet so many fascinating people and, for a little time at least, enter a world that may be very different from your own – a world which you might otherwise have no opportunity of sampling. Make yourself an observer of people and, above all, a listener.

That an interviewer must be keenly interested in the interviewee almost goes without saying but plunge into it with insufficient thought and it may become a nightmare. Your preparation must be thorough. Practical considerations come first. How long is the interview to be? When? Where will it take place? Will there be accompanying pix taking some of 'your' space? Does the editor want a particular type of interview, or is it assumed that you know the market and how to write for it?

Setting up the interview

This is really not too difficult to do provided you are not trying to get an interview with someone at the very top of his tree – for whatever reason he happens to be there. Attempt to set up an interview with, say, the American President on one of his rare trips to the UK and you'll only be wasting your time, not his. He won't even know you exist. The best approach to someone less exalted – but equally newsworthy from your market's point of view – is to find out who acts as his spokesman (if he can't be contacted directly): a member of his family, his publicist (the modern term for public relations manager), agent, publisher, manager or whoever keeps him in the forefront of the public eye.

Telephone at a reasonable time of day and ask if it is a convenient moment to talk. Assuming it is, state who you are, which paper you are working for and why you would like to arrange an interview. Give brief details of what your readers would like and if you already have pieces published, say so. This helps establish your credibility and gives your subject the opportunity to check your credentials if he is at all suspicious. In reality I have seldom found any great difficulty in securing an interview. Most people are only too willing to help out when they realise that they will be reaping the benefits of some free publicity.

Sometimes you may need to make contact more than once to secure the interview you want. At the first call the interviewee or his spokesman may be cautious and unwilling to give a definite answer. At the second, people may be more relaxed than they were at the first. Be very careful when making appointments over the telephone. Check and double-check the venue, the time, the person's likes and dislikes about voice-recorders and so on – and determine how long your interviewee imagines the interview will last.

What if he declines? Only you can decide whether a refusal means he's just playing hard to get and will give in if you're more persistent, he's learned to be wary of newspaper journalists (yes, when a few behave despicably, as they do, we all suffer), or he genuinely does not want any publicity. In the tough and uncompromising world of newspapers some journalists will urge you be ruthless, to ignore pleas for privacy and to hit hard if you want to succeed, regardless of other people's wishes. Maybe you can – and will. I can't.

It is seldom necessary to obtain written consent when someone agrees to be interviewed. If he's in the public eye, his secretary or publicist will have a note of it – although you may like to confirm your part of the agreement in writing to ensure there are no mistakes regarding everything that has been agreed. The less well-known sometimes like to help with research in the interests of their own publicity; this is quite acceptable as long as there is no onus on you to feature any particular aspect of their lives or work.

Where and when?

Circumstances will dictate the best time to approach your interviewee for consent to the interview. You may be able to make the agreement first, with date, hour and place all arranged, and then begin your preparatory work; or you may fear that your interviewee will decline unless you can show some evidence of having done at least some of your homework at the first approach. Only you can choose the most propitious time to contact him. Whatever you decide remember some folk will be scared at the very word 'interview' but could respond favourably if you were to ask if they would like to 'talk' to you for the paper. Explain who you are, which paper will be publishing your interview (or you hope will be publishing it, if you are not yet commissioned), why you want to talk to him, about what, and indicate that you will readily fit in with his plans concerning dates, times, the length of the interview and so on. When arranging a time for the interview do check that your subject does actually have the time to spend talking to you. Twenty minutes just before a busy ophthalmologist is leaving for a hospital is not a good time to work on an in-depth feature on the latest developments in eye surgery.

You also need to make sure that your place of interview is reasonably quiet. It is important to opt for the best time and place for the interview (if you are in a position to choose) for both frequently affect the result. An interview over a meal is not to be recommended unless you are skilled at balancing plates with pens and notebooks, eating, drinking, asking questions and recording the answers all at the same time. Quiet country pubs may be good venues for seeing the interviewee loosen up and – perhaps – drop a few confidences, but it could be that the privacy of his house is a better venue. Accommodating his wishes is kindly and could make him feel well disposed towards you, but meeting at a place where you are not likely to be disrupted by outside influences is more sensible. Combine the two for optimum effect. Whatever the venue, ask how long your interviewee would like the interview to last. Very often you will find that if the interview goes well, it will last longer than your interviewee intended it should. This can only be to your advantage.

Research

Early hunters knew they had to feel the spirit of their prey before hunting began. They learned that doing so put them at an advantage – they understood their victims and learned how their minds and instincts worked. This is our interview research. Be certain in your own mind just what you want to find out about your interviewee, remembering that this will be what your readers will want to read. What question would they want to ask if they were conducting the interview?

Try and find out as much background information as you can about the person you are interviewing and the topic you are covering. It almost goes without saying that your research into his background must be comprehensive and undertaken with persistence. Don't stop finding out all you can about him until you are fully satisfied there is nothing relevant left to discover. As a freelance you will be held responsible for the accuracy of any information that appears in print regarding your interviewee. We freelances must remember that while the paper publishing our interviews may (or may not) check our facts, it is up to us, not the paper, to make sure everything contained in interviews is accurate. And it's not just a matter of getting the *facts* correct, important though that is. Remember the secret of those successful hunters – get to know your victim, even before you meet him.

Only a poor (and often uncommissioned) interviewer wastes time at the interview by asking questions he could have found answers to before the interview began. Unbeknown to your interviewee, therefore, you will be delving into his past. The more you find out about him, his background, family, career, likes, dislikes and anything else you can discover, the greater your confidence will be when you meet him face to face.

Make use of research material that is uniquely relevant to your interviewee. His friends working in his field of expertise, for example, with the same hobbies or shared experiences, may be able to give you information not to be found in any book. At the very least they will guide you on the vocabulary and basic knowledge of his special subject or achievement; without some grasp of what he may talk about you could soon find yourself out of your depth.

Cuttings already published about him will be valuable and may include previous interviews containing useful information. Perhaps he refers to a favourite sport or leisure occupation, or personal details may be revealed. Press releases may be available. Gather all information in your private notes regardless, at this stage, of how you might or might not make use of it. (Later, when you are more experienced in interviewing skills, you may have enough confidence to tackle the problem of selection as you do your research.) All your research and everything anybody tells you will provide you with a better basis for evaluation – and give you an increasingly logical perspective on the questions you may ask.

Research is like an iceberg in that nine-tenths of it will be hidden. It can be helpful to let a tenth show, for when you first approach your interviewee he will probably feel flattered on realising you have taken the trouble to do at least some homework about him. Later, during the course of the interview itself, the time and effort you have invested in preparation will prove its worth. So don't skimp on interview research; it may involve a lot of work but the more thoroughly it is done the easier and more pleasant will be the interview that follows.

Planning questions

Your interviewee and the research you've uncovered will greatly influence the pattern you choose, but your chosen market is the ruling hand in all your writing and remains so in preparing for an interview.

An old-fashioned formula was to compile questions more or less chronologically, beginning with childhood and family life then continuing with career-start and progress, problems, achievements and so on, according to what is relevant. This method still has its place as long as the pace doesn't drag (and it nearly always does) but for many papers there is neither space nor reading-time to tell the interviewee's whole story. The average reader's attention-span is limited and if the first few words of the interview don't catch him he'll turn his eyes elsewhere. What is it that makes your interviewee of interest to readers at that time? A single aspect of his eventful life or an important piece of knowledge he can provide on a topical issue? How to plan which questions to ask will be determined by this circumscription.

Generally it is not a good idea to ask anything controversial at the beginning. I usually work the plan into some sort of shape by writing down key questions as I think of them or as a particular item of research prompts me, on a large sheet of lined paper – leaving three or four lines between each question. This gives me room for more questions subsidiary to the main ones or lets me chop and change my first thoughts about as much as I like (and I always do). The flow of questions should vary in length, complexity and perhaps most of all in weight. Thoughtful and caring questions indicate your genuine interest in your interviewee and his theme and encourage him to expand on what he really thinks and feels – which is just what you want to hear. A relaxed atmosphere leads him to speak more freely and informally; ideally an interview should read like a spontaneous conversation. Questions that are predictable, dull or boring merely invite replies in the same vein, perhaps with disastrous results.

Begin by making a list of questions that you want to ask your subject. A few general questions at first will relax him (and you) and help establish mutual rapport. These I write out in lowercase because they are not important to my feature. With more experience you probably won't need to write these out at all as you will instinctively judge when the right moment comes along to begin the interview proper. My main questions that will form the subject of my feature or news piece I always write in uppercase (capitals) to remind me that these are the important questions I need answers for. I leave plenty of space under each question so I can note down the reply.

If he is a well-known figure you may find a formidable amount of information about him, saddling you with a bundle of notes far too large to handle during the interview. You can't ask every question that occurs to you and selection raises its worrying head. Which aspects of his life or work can you safely omit? This is where a good memory, even a short-term one, is a blessing. Perhaps you, like me, daren't rely on it – so improvise with tiny *aides-memoire* in your notes to jog you if the conversation wanders away from the track you've planned for it. Looking up some of my notes for interviewing an elderly artist I find 'Normandy' and 'Boots' which were enough to remind me he had lost the hearing in one ear on the Normandy beaches, and that he was a distant member of the family firm of the ubiquitous high-street chemists.

When I've shaped my questions as I think best I write them out again, and if I'm relying on shorthand or written notes I leave plenty of space after each question for the interviewee's reply. At an interview I also keep beside me a second sheet of paper reminding me about questions of lesser importance, and this second sheet has a assurance value. I fancy I will remember the relevant basic facts about my man and they may not be directly referred to in the course of the interview – but if they are and I've forgotten, I have my second sheet. In these image-conscious days people who are interviewed frequently, particularly in high-circulation papers, sometimes have special trainers to teach them the skills required to be a good interviewee. No longer do these high-powered media folk rely on their memories and mood at the time of an interview.

The interview

How should you greet your interviewee? With a handshake? If he advances and offers his hand, yes; otherwise probably no. You can tell a lot from a handshake and how easily he makes eye-contact with you. Does he grasp your hand with both of his? Do his fingers barely touch yours? If he doesn't offer his hand, is he inevitably going to be hard to interview? If you haven't pre-arranged the interview (because circumstances didn't permit it, perhaps) ask if it is convenient for him to answer some questions before you plunge right in. Remember you are not there to be the star so do not dress flamboyantly or give an appearance of being too pleased with yourself.

Generally an unobtrusive style of dress is best. But of course if you are interviewing a pop-star known for his casual dress and lack of formality, you would be wise not to be too formal in your appearance or approach.

Knowing you've arrived (promptly) with the tools of the trade gives you confidence: a notebook, your prepared and/or semi-prepared questions, a pen or pencil (and a couple of spares) and your portable voice-recorder if you plan to use one. There are many good models available which are inexpensive and easy to work, and using one will free you from having to take your eyes off your interviewee and his surroundings. Whatever machine you use, reliability is paramount or the entire interview could be lost. This is the sort of thing you might have nightmares about but such anxieties are nothing to the horror that can happen when you're wide awake. You must be totally familiar with how your recorder works and how long it will record for. I depend on a voice-recorder (Voice-It) that has a voice-activated control if required and will later transcribe my words (and his) straight onto my computer screen at the touch of a button. Whether you use a machine with a tape or without, any mid-interview fiddling is embarrassing and guaranteed to break the thread of what your interviewee might be thinking and saying. Remember, too, that tapes can be tampered with and do not make wholly reliable evidence of what was said if disputes arise. A recorder can do more than record the human voice. You can use it to observe surroundings, check the atmosphere of a place, determine the mood of your interviewee, and make private notes about any points or matters that he might wish – or not wish – to discuss.

Apart from modern gadgetry, take a suitable notebook. I prefer one with spiral binding on the left rather than at the top, the latter being too easily opened the wrong way up when you start note-taking. Spiral binding on the left ensures you write as in a normal exercise book and is less likely to cause any problems either during the interview or when you come to read back your notes. Also take with you proof of your identity or a copy of the paper you are working for if your interviewee doesn't already know you. A mobile phone is reassuring if you're not sure where the venue is or how to get to it. Don't forget spare batteries and film if you are using a voice-recorder or taking photographs.

Don't be late. Most people find it irritating and a sign of bad manners. If you are not sure of the address then ask for directions when you make arrangements for the interview. Arriving late and in a flustered state is not the best beginning and you won't impress your interviewee with your lack of professionalism. Make some small talk first – but not too much. This will give him time to assess how tough your questions are going to be and how he's going to handle the interview.

Try to make sure he enjoys it. Do that and you will end up with a far more natural and interesting interview for your readers, so don't be impatient or react adversely to anything he says, no matter how provoking. Be sympathetic even if you don't feel it. Let him think you are on his side. Shed any presumptions you might have and try to remember that empathy is about showing you understand your interviewee's problems. You want to get something out of him so a degree of rapport is necessary, even if it can't always be entirely genuine. Strangely, after a job well done there might be a certain amount of grudging respect in the air; you may even have softened his earlier opinion about you and the paper you stand for.

Resist bringing all your armoury out at once and laying it on the table – an action enough to frighten all but the most robust interviewee. Ask if he is happy with the use of a recorder (unless you have already established this point when you arranged for the interview to take place) and produce your tools casually over the first few moments while you're talking in a friendly manner before the interview begins. He won't agree? Undoubtedly some people are inhibited by the realisation that a bit of electronic wizardry is remorselessly docketing their every breath. If this happens you'll have to rely on your own writing; the weeks or months you spent learning shorthand will pay dividends and with practice the speed of your best scribble will increase. I can't over-emphasise the value of learning shorthand even though it now seems an old-fashioned skill. Modern devices have their uses (and you won't find a keener enthusiast for them than me) but they do not and cannot replace shorthand in every situation. If you will be taking notes by hand have your notebook comfortably in your hand or on your lap rather than on a desk or table. You will be able to relax more easily and (more importantly) your eyes will have less distance to travel between your notes and your interviewee's face so you will not be constantly dropping and lifting your head. Even keeping your subject in the corner of your eye while you write on your notepad can be revealing; the less jerkiness there is between question and answer, the more natural the conversation will be, and the smoother the interview. Remind him of how long you agreed the interview should last. Put your watch on the table if you will be able to see it less obtrusively there, or keep it on your wrist if you can look at it without him noticing.

As the interview begins make sure you can see both him and your notebook clearly especially if daylight has faded or will fade before you've finished. Speak clearly so he can hear you without any difficulty and concentrate. When you are both settled it will be up to you to set the interview rolling. Don't let it roll for long before establishing your theme, i.e. what you're there for, what it is that's going to interest your readers about this man, and what he's going to say about it. Start calmly and confidently and if appropriate remember that a little gentle flattery or praise never goes amiss.

Beware of having the tables turned on you by a skilful and experienced interviewee. If the questions are not to his liking or he wishes to be mischievous, he may begin asking *you* questions instead of answering yours. Don't let this happen. A smile is all you may allow yourself and perhaps a little shake of the head but don't say anything about yourself or attempt to answer his questions. Your readers want to hear about him, not you.

Try to make as few notes as you can. It is fatal to be so busy taking down what is said that your interviewee thinks you are more interested in getting it down than paying attention to what he is saying. Notes are just to remind you, with verbatim note-taking reserved for quotes and very important replies.

Keep your cool

If you've never met your interviewee before it can be difficult to keep your mind on the job at the beginning. It is quite natural to be a little nervous; some interviewers, like some actors, claim it keeps the adrenalin flowing for optimum performance. Once I interviewed a stage star who was well aware he was a good-looker. Long accustomed to admiration, he turned on the charm and kept it going throughout the interview. I managed (with difficulty) to play along with his vanity, mindful of my task – and the result was an interview that pleased everyone.

Interesting quotes are most likely to come from people who are lively, intelligent and interested in what they do. And what they do will probably be the reason for you interviewing them in the first place. Charm and looks don't make a good interview; what the interviewee says is what readers want to know. Do a great deal more than listen to the words. Observe your interviewee's clothes, for instance, for how he dresses shows a great deal about his character. Whatever the clothing, notice whether he is comfortable in it. If he is, he will be much more relaxed and you will get a better interview. Notice jewellery. Is it expensive, sentimental or brash? And grooming comes into the same category as dress. Observe it carefully and let it help you in both the questions you ask and the way in which you ask them.

Always try to be relaxed in your attitude and remember you are conducting an interview, not an interrogation. It is best to be friendly (but not too familiar) and not to be so keen to frame your next question that you don't listen to what he's saying. Spot other points, too, that give you information without being put into words. Just as your attitude and tone of voice will affect the interview, particularly at the beginning, so will his. Listen to his body language as well as his words. Experts will tell you that crossing the knees towards another person is a sign of acceptance or interest. Gestures with glasses or cigarettes and fidgeting with hair or jewellery can be very revealing if you know how to interpret them.

Always be ready to rephrase questions if the way you had intended to ask them does not seem appropriate when they arise. If you cannot get an answer, or what you consider to be a satisfactory answer, to a particularly tricky question never resort to veiled threats. 'So I can tell readers you won't answer . . . ' will only antagonise an already reluctant interviewee who feels himself forced into a corner. Most of all, avoid paraphrasing what he has said with 'So you are saying . . . '. The first (and only) time I tried this I was coldly told, 'No. You are saying that.'

Avoid asking either/or questions. 'Did you know you were going to be asked to take over the Minister's job that morning or was it a total surprise?' 'Yes,' he answers. Reading your notes or listening to the tape later you wonder which part of the question received the answer 'Yes.' Confusion reigns. Ask double-sided questions such as this and any celebrity used to being interviewed will spot your error. He could reply 'Yes' with the latter part of your question in mind, he could be letting you fall into your own trap, or he might just not care what he replied to such a poorly phrased question.

Guard against subconsciously steering your questions in a direction that will later ease the writing of the interview (unless they naturally fall in such a pattern) and don't be frightened to acknowledge a mistake if you make one. If you find yourself inserting extra questions that didn't occur to you until you're face to face, fine. You're relaxing with a natural sincerity that will be welcomed and matched in spontaneous replies. For he may also have been nervous when you started.

Always remember you are in charge. He is more important than you are, but you are in charge of the interview. You've set it up, prepared for it, and you are going to have it printed in the newspaper. On this last point, he may be a little anxious. After all, he wants something good written about him in your newspaper and he is keen to make a good impression on you. If you admit to him that you don't understand something he has answered to one of your questions or a point he is talking about he is likely to be flattered. Express curiosity and confess to being intrigued by his replies when and where appropriate, without taking the conversation off its intended track. This makes him feel good and he will become easier to interview.

A woman whose husband had left her only hours after their wedding told me she only wanted to be interviewed so she could shame him in public. A man thought an interview about his house (which was like many others) would help him sell it. Not everyone sees interviews as we do. But on the whole, interviewees are helpful, attentive – and cautious. I've always made an effort to look at a forthcoming interview from the interviewee's point of view, and very often this has helped both of us. Barely replying to any questions, a shy young violinist couldn't even look at me as we began the interview he had agreed to in his garden. We seemed to be getting nowhere when he said, 'I can only talk through my fingers.' He started to play and a powerful wave of emotion rose and fell over the quiet garden. He paused and began telling me about his return to his beloved instrument after an accident damaging his hand. Gently, with bursts of violin playing, he gave a sensitive and moving account of his recovery. The interview might have been an ordeal for him; it was a privilege for me.

With the interview going well you'll understand why I say interviewing is so enjoyable. Let him do the talking and only guide the drift or intervene to ask questions. You'll find yourself seizing unexpected openings, earning unforeseen bonuses with, perhaps, a confession of your own ignorance or an extra depth of understanding, and all the time you're at the centre of a fascinating and often heart-warming conversation. Even though this is a deliberately set-up interview, being genuine is at the heart of all worthwhile communication. As people vary enormously, you may find some interviewees positively expand once the interview is underway. Just as friends can talk together half jokingly, so can an interviewee in response to what he might otherwise see as questions rather too close to the knuckle.

With a light and apparently innocent touch, you are guiding but never forcing him towards the answers you hope he'll make. Push him and he may dry up on you. Be aggressive and he'll prickle. Being in charge does not mean being inflexible for sticking doggedly to your plan could make you miss those informal gems he'll let slip when he's at ease. At such times, often late in the interview, there may be a moment to ask a 'risky' question almost as if you've only just thought of it – and that is when he might give you some of your most valuable information.

Noticing whether people use a lot of words or long words, whether they speak with authority or whether they are unsure of themselves will in due course help you to become a more perceptive and sensitive interviewer and guide you towards getting the best results from anyone you interview. Sometimes a moving recollection or response is best greeted with nothing more than a nod or a gentle smile for there is a time to keep silent in most interviews. He could need a short break (and so could you) to recover himself and as long as it doesn't last too long this can be useful. While he organises a cup of tea, lights a cigarette or just blows his nose, you will be catching up on what's gone so far and what's coming next.

If your subject has agreed to be photographed, it's usually best to take the pix at the end of the interview. It is a good way of rounding things off and he will be well used to you by then and more amenable to your instructions. There are exceptions to this guidance. The light may be just right on your arrival or you may know that the house will be bursting with unruly children by the time you finish. In these cases take the photographs first, even if you have to use a little more skill to coax your subject to relax.

Surprises

Enjoyable as interviewing nearly always is, you are there to do a job and nothing better can drop into your lap than a revelation. Your interviewee springs some big news: he's left his wife, he's giving up the job that made him famous – whatever, in his context, is news. Suddenly you have a news story as well. It can't be wasted in an interview that might not be printed before next week and you have all the research material about your man at your fingertips. It sometimes happens that an interviewee lets slip an unguarded remark or comment that he almost immediately wishes to retract. He may apologise, be embarrassed and ask you to ignore what he said. You can only be guided by circumstances but with the sincerity of a genuine mistake having been made it is sensible to agree to his retraction in most cases. To fall into the trap (as some media interviewers do) of pouncing on such slips with glee is poor technique and unlikely to benefit anyone. Your interviewee will be upset and whatever co-operative attitude you may have established will instantly be lost.

A request that you should keep a particular statement 'off the record' is not quite the same. I dislike being put in this position for I am being asked to lay aside the interviewer's hat and – for a few moments, perhaps – to be a personal friend. It's not that I don't want to be friendly (I usually do) but the interviewee is suddenly and unjustly assuming control of the interview. For decency's sake I am obliged to observe whatever confidentiality is to be kept, and do so, albeit the interviewee has taken advantage of me and my position.

If the interviewee sees or suspects you are not making a good job of the interview (for lack of skill, i.e. shorthand, note-taking, because you haven't done your preparation adequately or are just too nervous to do a good job) he will worry about what might appear in print – and that itself will make him nervous of what he says and how much he reveals.

At the close of an interview as well as thanking him for his time and help I like to spend a few minutes winding things down with a little more general conversation. This helps to keep things on an informal, friendly level in the hope that both of us feel quite content about what has taken place.

Writing it up

Your deadline may determine how soon you write up your interview but even if you are not under such pressure I advise doing it as soon as possible while it's still fresh in your head. This gets the job done, leaves you free for other work and lessens the danger of involuntarily imagining that something was said when it wasn't. Did he mention such-and-such which you didn't write down or has the thought supplanted the words because you hoped to hear them? Be careful about what you think he said, what he actually said, what you think you heard him say, what he may have meant by what he said and what your later thoughts lead you to believe he actually *did* mean by what he said. Consider how his replies to your questions were or were not an indicator of what he really felt. Every interviewer soon learns to become something of a psychologist as well.

Of course you will write the interview up in the way in which your chosen publication likes it. We're back to market study, never forgetting that the whole purpose of conducting the interview is to get across to the reader why the person you're interviewing is worth listening to and why they will enjoy reading about him. You take home a bundle of notes, a couple of full tapes and a headful of images; you can hear his voice, visualise his mannerisms and feel his friendliness (or otherwise). How is all this to be translated into a written interview?

Recall that your job is for a newspaper, which means catching the readers' attention immediately. Consulting your original draft for the interview may give you some of your structure, but setting to work very soon after the interview will provide you with a fresher, closer and brighter start; indeed you may decide to abandon all your first thoughts and intentions. The enthusiasm and spontaneity that rubs off a charismatic interviewee is invaluable in seeing you through the writing-up of the interview, as long as you keep your feet on the ground. You were there and your readers were not; your task is to make them feel they had been.

As with any other piece of written work it is important to make a strong start. Did your interviewee say anything to make a good opening quote? Try something strong at the beginning, establish the topical peg (if that is the purpose of the interview) and reveal why and where the interview is taking place. Perhaps give an idea of what the interviewee looks like and one or two other individual points about him, but beware of letting such an intro turn into waffle. As with all writing for newspapers, the start of the piece must be the start of the story, not some preamble *about* it. 'I love getting married. It's being married I don't like,' was my intro to an interview with a thrice-divorced actress currently dating a youngster half her age. This had been her answer to a question she had mused about without any prompting from me. 'I suppose you wonder who my next will be?' Her eyes undressed my paper's 45-year-old photographer and flickered away. His face was a better picture than any he'd ever taken. Another good opening might be something that made you laugh during the interview, recorded either directly or indirectly, or an aspect of the interviewee that particularly moved you and will move readers. Don't forget you can also use flashbacks as long as they do not take over the main stream of the write-up.

How much of 'you' is there going to be and how are you going to present yourself? Are you to appear as a friend, a colleague or just a disembodied and unidentified voice? And how are the questions to be posed – every one in direct quotes ('What do you most want in life?') or occasionally dropping into indirect speech ('I asked him what he most wanted in life.') to avoid monotony? On the whole nothing makes an interview more alive on the published page than direct quotes; bearing the balance of the copy in mind, the more you can include the better and for these you'll bless your voice-recorder. Writing all or part of the interview in the present tense may also keep it light with a friendly impact. Beware, nonetheless, of being too informal, lest readers feel you have treated your interviewee flippantly – especially if the theme, i.e. why you are interviewing him, is of a sensitive or serious nature.

When sprinkled throughout an article, the personal attributes of people you interview can give it life that spoken words cannot provide. Words that are not spoken may also reveal a lot about character. It is a good idea to keep an important quote to the end. This will be a good rounding-off and give a feeling of satisfaction to your readers.

Done! But . . .

You've finished. The write-up is complete and you're ready to file it to the paper. Did your interviewee say anything about wanting to see what you've written before it's published? It is best to make it clear that you will only alter incorrect facts such as statistics. It's a tricky point and I well understand the temptation of letting him vet what you have written before it gets into cold print. That way, you might comfort yourself, there will be no complaints, denials or misunderstandings about what he did or did not say or mean. What he wants deleted can be cut out, in other places you can amend your copy to accommodate his second (or third) thoughts and anything he would like rephrased is easily altered. Above all, you'll be in the clear.

Resist, please. If, for instance, he doesn't have an exact reference at his fingertips while you're talking to him and would like you to include it you would be unreasonable to refuse him the chance of making a later addition. But in normal circumstances, holding back on the idea of letting an interviewee revise your copy is not due to stubborn pride or any sense of superiority about what you've written. It is a practical matter. Imagine the delays if all copy had to be checked, possibly in long-winded detail, by the people it concerned; however would the paper get printed in time? There's another reason: to let your copy be 'passed' by someone who is hardly the best judge of what he may have said about himself will be undermining your credibility. If we don't learn to take interviews and do any other newspaper jobs and then practise and polish our skills we will of no substantial value to any newspaper. That doesn't mean our early interviewees must be sacrificed to our own career-interests – just the reverse. Knowing (or assuming) that the interviewer is capable and confident of doing a good job will give greater confidence to an interviewee as well.

Keep all the notes and tapes you have made for at least a year after your story is published just in case any legal or court action is ever brought against you or your newspaper. The Defamation Act of 1966 defines the length of time (currently one year) within which this must be done. Since an important case in 1999 when former Irish Prime Minister Albert Reynolds sued the *Sunday Times* and received one penny in damages, freelances have been particularly vigilant. There is no safer protection than getting the facts right. Staff journalists can usually rely on editors to put the legal stamp on copy, but the onus is entirely on the shoulders of a freelance.

A sting in the tail?

Do your very best to avoid trouble, and complaints can still occasionally arise after an interview is published. 'I've been misquoted!' 'That's not true!' There is little to be done when this happens. No editor wants to be involved in disputes and it could boil down to taking your interviewee's word or yours. You have your notes or tapes to support you if necessary, but the editor is the arbiter and he should be your ultimate support. He knows you, your reliability and your standard of work. Yes, he knows you can also make mistakes; you are human, as is your interviewee. Unless matters reach a crisis (which seldom happens) nothing official will be done other than sending a polite reply to the interviewee regretting the receipt of his complaint; you may never even know there was one.

Perhaps is it the unpredictability of interviewing that gives it that special satisfaction but I can't pretend that the surprises you might encounter are unfailingly welcome. Unwanted distractions can wreak havoc with your carefully planned half-hour. Your interviewee may fancy a couple of floppy spaniels on the sofa, a background of fortissimo Wagner and boisterously inexhaustible toddlers given free access to the interview; how tolerant should you be? A wife/mother/secretary may break in with messages, requests and general diversions; do you smile gamely through them all for fear of upsetting your interviewee? That is another reason for fixing your interview location as tactfully as you can in the first place. A friendly greeting or pat on the head to interruptors on two or four legs is one thing: an interviewee constantly distracted and not properly listening to your questions or giving merely surface responses may mean a ruined interview.

Sometimes those seasoned in the business of being interviewed arrange the 'multi-interview'. You have assumed it will be a one-to-one affair, but no; you arrive to discover that a 'minder' or two is to sit in the room with you, perhaps even answering up for your interviewee or fending off questions he doesn't like. Usually in these circumstances you won't be the only interviewer either so the event resembles a mini press conference more than an interview. If you do find this happening to you, without any forewarning or contrary to what you have been led to believe would occur, it is generally best to cut your losses and leave. You won't be missing much for any exclusivity will be lost. A press release about your potential interviewee will supply whatever your editor might want to see, if he's still interested; but a write-up from a press release is very different from the result of a live interview.

Where a child is involved as an interviewee, or in an important supporting role, it is expected that a parent or adult will be present. In these circumstances you will have to trust that the adult does not interfere or restrict the course of your questioning, and rely on your own reserves of gentleness with the child and patience with the adult.

A top newspaper interviewer told me that only once during more than 40 years of interviewing had he been threatened about what he must or must not write. He demurred, the threat was repeated more sternly and my colleague walked out. No interview was published.

One extra task remains to be done after the interview is published. Write a brief 'thank you' note to your interviewee and slip in a copy of the published interview in case he hasn't seen it. If you haven't time to do this you could give your interviewee a quick ring when the piece appears in print. This is very much appreciated by those who may not be subscribers to the particular paper you are targeting.

Telephone interviewing

It sounds easy; conduct your interview over the telephone. There's no time wasted getting to a pre-arranged venue (and back), no worrying about what to wear (formal, casual or what?), no fear of not having taken everything you need – and the whole job is done quickly and effectively. Quickly, yes, but effectively? I doubt it.

Interviewing by phone and even by correspondence is often done but in my opinion nothing beats going and seeing for yourself. The best interviews get 'inside' interviewees, which leaves telephone interviews out in the cold. A conversation by correspondence may be a little closer to the real thing. Yet in both these circumstances the word 'interview' takes on a different meaning. One may be the only way you can get a direct quote; the other could be a legitimate avenue of research for a personal profile – and both are perfectly valid means of communication. But unless you are extremely talented and/or experienced, neither will capture the impact and immediacy that gives your published copy sparkle and makes your readers feel they, too, were talking to the famous. Think of the times when you've tried to talk to someone who will not look you in the face – not at a time of an official interview but just in general conversation. Lack of eye-contact makes personal communication very hard. A similar difficulty arises when someone you are talking to wears glasses so dark you cannot see his eyes. You cannot judge his reaction to the conversation, or even whether he is looking at you and listening to what you are saying. In a face-to-face interview it is even harder. If your interviewee can see into your eyes but you cannot see into his, you are at a disadvantage. 'But on the telephone,' you might point out, 'he can't see into my eyes either.' That's true. But choosing to interview him by telephone, in a situation where you cannot see his facial expressions and reactions, you (who should be in control of the interview) are deliberately putting a barrier between yourself and your interviewee.

Nevertheless there will be some occasions when only an interview by telephone is possible for reasons of distance, speed or convenience – or because the person you want to interview declines being interviewed in any other way. Then it's time to use the best aspects telephone interviewing presents and not get bogged down with the disadvantages.

If he is of a normally reserved character, your telephone interviewee may more readily let slip information about himself or the subject in question than he would have done were he looking you in the eye. Perhaps he finds it easier to swank a little about himself or his achievements, not having to look you in the face or to let you see the mannerisms that would reveal more than he might like them to. No inner sense can tell you, over the phone, whether he is mischievously exaggerating or deliberately misleading you. The other side of the telephone-interview coin is that you can't see your interviewee's reaction to your questions – his facial response which often reveals more than his words.

On the phone there will be only that curious talking-in-turns that telephones inflict on us for small talk or to allow either of you to catch your breath or take stock of the questions and answers. You won't have a chance to admire the garden or sip at your coffee. Such apparent diversions create useful 'space' for you to think quickly about new questions, or how to turn the talking back to where you want it, should it have 'drifted' a little. In face-to-face interviews, little breathing spaces can be put to good use. But the telephone is a demanding ear all its own: keep silent and you may be thought ill-mannered or your interviewee may think you don't like or approve of what he last said – and that might not be what you want at all.

> *There's so much good in the worst of us and so much bad in the best of us,*
> *That it hardly becomes any of us to talk about the rest of us.*
> (Anon)

8. Research

I don't know about you, but I came into this world knowing nothing at all: I had a few natural instincts, maybe, but absolutely nothing in the way of knowledge or understanding. That means that everything I have ever learned or understood in my life was originally the knowledge or understanding acquired or worked out by someone else. Now my head is full of information in great variety and I understand many things, although not as many as I would like to. So where did all this knowledge come from? It came from other people. And whatever you know or understand – that came from other people too.

Of course we don't call this plagiarism, defining that as the calculated and lazy way of profiting from someone else's research work as if we had done it ourselves. But that we all, every day, use information originally unearthed by someone else is indisputable – just as most of them in their turn took it from their predecessors. We call it learning. When we set about extending our knowledge to feed our writing projects we are taking steps to a greater understanding. Research means going the extra yard, delving more deeply into the information required, enriching our own understanding of our topic – and then presenting it to readers in our own way. And its greatest value is not the gathering of more facts, important as that is, but that we can give back to readers a deeper understanding of the topic because we ourselves have learned to understand it better.

Before you've had anything published in a newspaper (and especially if you are beginning to fear you never will) you may think established freelances have a secret recipe hidden from you. Only when you get to know a few more closely do you have an inkling of what goes on behind the scenes. Maybe you'll never discover how many books they have to consult to find a single piece of information, that an obscure statistic took three months to track down, where they came across a fascinating anecdote, or how they manage to interview celebrities who have hitherto refused to speak to the press. You don't hear about their cuttings files painstakingly garnered over the years or their precious 'contacts' books of people who can tell them what they want to know – or at least point them in the right direction to finding out. Oh yes, established freelances certainly have recipes and because they have worked long and hard to make them *individually* valuable they will guard them closely and keep them secret.

In the same way much of the help you gather round you as your writing life progresses will also be personal and of use only to you. Your own book of contacts, for instance, is worth a great deal. It will carry names of people you've found who can and will provide you with valuable information, listed with where to find them and just what help they provide. I am no artist but I know where to turn for essential artwork or pix in a hurry. Or I can be confident that if my contacts can't help me quickly, one of them will know someone else who can. Often one contact will lead you to another in this way, and so your contacts increase and the book becomes even more valuable. Parting journalists from their contacts books is worse than robbing babies of their milk.

Cuttings files

Second only to a contacts book in a do-it-yourself system come your private files of cuttings. These grow to enormous size as you snip and collect bits of information you hear, read about or gather somehow (some of the ways this may be done are discussed below). Very soon your files will become your best friends, because nobody will have exactly the same ones to refer to. I'm not saying you'll be at a disadvantage if you quote the same facts as other journalists (facts are facts after all) but if you can support your quotes from your own cuttings files your copy will stand out as at least sharp and at best unique. Building your own files is not difficult; many writers are compulsive collectors of snippets of information long before they've thought about what use they're likely to be. Every newspaper you read, every book or magazine that comes before you, everything anyone says that just might come in handy, you either snip it out, copy it in your notebook or jot it down on the back of your hand. Easy, isn't it? Yes, until . . .

Stuff it all into an old cardboard box and one day you'll have to sort it out and decide how much is useful and what may be discarded (my discard pile is always so small when I sort out cuttings that I generally decide not to throw anything away after all). Tidiness is not the only reason for keeping your cuttings in order: every item should be dated and sourced before you put it away. If you're collecting willy-nilly you may prefer to ignore the last instruction and fill the cardboard box with everything, promising yourself you'll have a grand sort out at a later date. Fair enough, if you wish. But I still advise preparing departmentalised cuttings files and putting your cherished cuttings in the right place at the start. It doesn't matter how primitive your files are; old envelopes clearly labelled but held together with a rubber band or in a shoe box will serve the purpose. Better and easier to manage are concertina-type files with large identifiable pockets that are easily renamed. As your cuttings files enlarge you'll realise you need to make subdivisions of some sections, so off you branch into more envelopes, shoe boxes or concertina files. However you do it, keeping to an ordered system is one thing you'll have cause to bless frequently in the future.

On the cutting itself, remind yourself of your source – i.e. where you found it. This is important and can make the difference between a helpful and a doubtful cutting. Even more important is putting a date on it. Imagine that you dug out a cutting giving population figures in Manitoba, say, before 'last year's census'. The cutting has no date on it, so when was the census? How accurate are the quoted figures now? You don't know and you daren't (if you are wise) risk using it. There's only one thing to do with such a cutting: tear it up. You might be tempted to use it and could land yourself in trouble because you relied on the unreliable. Furthermore, it has wasted your time and space, so a cutting without a date is worse than no cutting at all.

I am so built that I cannot throw away any snippet of information or opinion I come across even if I don't want to use it for any current project – on the principle that if it interested me sufficiently to cut it out and keep it, it must surely be of interest to readers somewhere, some time. It's too good to cast aside, I tell myself, it's bound to come in useful . . . and sure enough in most cases it does. Who could throw away such apparently inconsequential gems as these, for instance? (If you want to make use of them yourself, feel free to do so; but before I use them – if and when I do – I will check that they are still valid and would advise you to do the same.)

- The world's termites outweigh the world's humans by 10 to 1.
- Pound for pound, in weight, hamburgers cost more then new cars.
- It's what you learn after you know it all that counts.
- Across Europe, almost 70% of children under 16 have mobile phones.
- The council said that the cemetery had to raise its burial charges due to the cost of living.
- The happiest people are those who think the happiest thoughts – and they also bring the greatest happiness to other people.

A last word about cuttings files: let them be your servants but not your masters. It's possible a cutting is incorrect. Whoever wrote it might have made a mistake; by relying on it without question you could be perpetuating that mistake. So check it, unless it's quite impossible to do so – in which case you must make a decision about whether or not to use it. If you decide not to risk it, something else in the file will set you off on another trail if you want one. Frankly, I can't imagine any writer could be short of inspiration when looking through cuttings, for my problem is having far too many with not enough time to use them. Your cuttings files will ensure you never run out of ideas.

Research and reference

Having decided on your topic and where you are going to send it you must ask yourself what you need to know. How much research must be done? The very word *research* means not to search, but to search *again*: to dig more deeply, to pass beyond what other people might find out about the topic – so that you can reveal new and interesting information to your readers. Make a list of all you need to find out by asking yourself a series of questions. Take my story about the man easily flooded with electricity (*see* page 47), and the questions might be:

- What *is* static electricity?
- What causes an excess of it?
- What is a normal amount to have or generate?
- Is it dangerous?
- If so, in what ways?
- Can it be eased or stopped?
- Are there famous cases of an excess of it?

These were the first questions I had to find answers for, and there were others. As I began talking to people, varied aspects of the topic grew in my head and put another question to me: how much of what I learned should I include and what should I leave out? Usually such decisions can only be made when I start writing. Some researched answers will fit in as entirely appropriate, while unwanted bits will not sit easily on the page. If you ever find yourself writing just to be able to use a researched fact, take another look at what you've written – and don't let the tail wag the dog.

A different approach to research was needed for answers to the questions 'What happened to the treasure said to have been lost by King John in a short cut across the Wash in 1215? What *was* it? Was it ever found? And if not, does modern technology for searching the sea bed allow us to find it now?'

A dip into my cuttings files reminds me that somewhere it is always the season of celebrating traditional practices up and down the country. In my locality the old custom of Morris dancing attracts many spectators. But how many folk know its origins and the reasons for its survival? I didn't until I researched the topic – and discovered its unusual history. What began as a fertility rite many thousands of years ago almost died out after the 1914–18 war, when so many dancers did not return (there are still no women allowed in traditional teams). Delving into this story I was at first doubtful of its appeal to modern readers.

History, of any sort, can be a deterrent to casual readers looking for entertainment. Personal touches were essential to 'lift' the copy, particularly at the start. Luckily I found plenty of dancers happy to talk about their stick-clicking hobby and one elderly man (no longer dancing) cheerfully recalled leading a dancing team through a barren field. 'No crops grew,' he grinned, 'but a bull got the message and escaped from the field to rampage among a group of heifers.' Start any light piece with a smile and you've broken any ice that might be forming.

Supposing you are writing a 'help' article and want to use an incident where a toddler went missing in a crowded shopping precinct. Could you advise readers what to do in such circumstances? How can you find out where to turn for help, whom to call first and the best way in which you – either as an observer or as a distraught parent – can assist the police and other helpers in finding the child as quickly as possible? These and many other questions will need answers – accurate, up-to-date answers – before you can think about how to write your piece. All you need to know in this and at the start of almost every project lies in a single word: research. In the first instance, that usually means consulting reference books.

Editors report that inadequate research is one of the main reasons for rejection – and sometimes, checking what you *thought* you knew is the first task, as I discovered from a little item in *Book News*. Like other readers I assumed 'haggis' to be Scottish: not so, apparently. A recipe for it appears in an eighteenth-century cookery book and it was known for hundreds of years in several parts of Europe. Another haggis bites the dust . . . But I still wouldn't use this information in copy without first checking it to my satisfaction.

Research can be fun. I was asked to compile a selection of children's sayings and laughed so much in doing so that I could hardly put fingers to keyboard.

- Noah's wife was called Joan of Ark.
- The name of the American flag is the Tarzan Stripes.
- In the Middle Ages, everyone was middle aged.
- Socrates took wedlock and died.
- The ancient Egyptians wrote in hydraulics.
- King Henry VIII made Wolsey a cardigan.

- A thesaurus was a monster thousands of years ago with a long neck.
- Mayonnaise is the French National Anthem.

Another assignment took me into more serious waters with sayings of a different type: truisms and pronouncements about life in general by worthy folk of the past. This was sobering: *The secret of man's being*, wrote Dostoyevsky, *is not only to live, but to have something to live for*. I also came across an unattributed saying that ran like this: *It has taken me all my life to understand it is not necessary to understand everything*.

Our source material for research lies mainly in books. There are several handbooks listing titles, addresses, phone numbers and other details about newspapers. Some are published annually so cannot keep pace with month-to-month, let alone day-to-day changes; that restriction apart, they are thorough and reliable. The essence of credibility is getting the facts correct so it is important to keep your method of research up-to-date. The following handbooks are virtually indispensable:

- *Research for Writers* (A & C Black, Alderman House, 37 Soho Square, London W1D 3QZ *tel* 020 7758 0200 *email* sales@acblack.com *website* www.acblack.com)
  The latest edition of this brilliant book by researcher Ann Hoffman is now a well-established tool of reference offering a wealth of first-class guidance and information. It is no exaggeration to describe it as essential to every serious writer. Through its pages you will be led to research in every field and merely reading *how* to pursue your particular trail will whet your appetite to begin.
- *Hollis* (Harlequin House, 7 High Street, Teddington, Middlesex TW11 8EL *tel* 020 8977 7711/020 8977 1133 *email* orders@hollis-pr.com *website* www.hollis-pr.com)
  Widely regarded as the 'bible of the industry', this is an expensive but unique reference book for researchers – and a goldmine of press and publicity contacts, story leads and ideas. With more than 20,000 entries, it points you in the right direction every time; a rich source of contacts for finding just about anything. Also published by Hollis are several other useful books of reference.

It is always worth consulting reference books published years ago as well as more recent arrivals on the scene. This being so, you may not easily find what you want. Here are some oldies I particularly recommend:

- *A Concise Dictionary of Confusables* (Hodder & Stoughton)
  Was the villain *hanged* on the gallows, or *hung*? Is *proficiency* the same as *efficiency*? Does *supine* mean *prone*? To settle these and any other confusions this is the book to buy.
- *The Concise Oxford Dictionary of Quotations*
- *The Concise Oxford Dictionary of Proverbs*
- *The Concise Oxford Dictionary of English Etymology*
  } Three for every writer's desk
- *Chambers Idioms*
  Another gem. The use of idioms and figurative expressions in our richly expressive language will lift your copy, enlivening your writing. But this book is more than a list of idioms; knowing the origins of many adds to a writer's understanding and ability to use them.
- *Chambers Dates*
  This book covers such a diversity of topics (politics, literature, sport, business, people, exploration – you name it and it's almost certainly here) that it's a fine prop for all seekers after general knowledge as well as a ready reference. With more than 6,000 important dates listed, there should be enough variety for us all.

The amount of information to be found on the internet is incalculable (*see* the next chapter for more details on how to find it) but needs to be viewed with care. Such an excess can stifle rather than enlighten and a special sort of discipline is called for in limiting one's selection – odd as that restriction may seem when talking about the apparently bottomless well of research. Information on compact disk is generally more manageable than that found on websites easily altered at the whim of the website manager.

For invaluable and totally reliable information nothing can match *Britannica CD* – the complete encyclopaedia on a single disk – in breadth of knowledge, quality of information and ease of use. It covers more than 65,000 subjects in articles ranging from concise explanations to comprehensive expositions; and from historical treatments of subjects to coverage of current events. There is quick access to word definitions from the 10th edition of the *Merriam-Webster's Collegiate Dictionary*, and close on half a million references have been compiled, edited and hypertext-linked to text articles for easy navigation. As well as this there are more than 10,000 links to pictures and tables. A powerful 'search-and retrieve engine' replaces the printed volumes to scan the 44-million-word database, presenting an almost unbelievable wealth of information on your screen.

Other CDs particularly helpful to writers are those covering specialist subjects such as anatomy, space travel, the history of the motor car and similar topics where the opinion and experience of acknowledged experts has been burned onto these shiny marvels of resource material.

Other help

What do you do if you know a book exists but you can't find it? (*See* also chapter 9.) Luckily for researchers there are folk who specialise in solving this very difficulty. They advertise their services in writers' publications or sometimes in the national or regional press. I can't vouch for the practical results of asking for help from any particular one but on the whole I have found that anyone offering this service is unlikely to advertise without a sound network of established contacts as the searcher earns nothing if unsuccessful. Always supply as much information as you can when in search of any book: the title and author, and if possible the date of publication and the publisher.

Library services

The refurbished Dome Reading Room of the Imperial War Museum (Lambeth Road, London SE1 6HZ *Printed Books* 020 7416 5344 *Documents* 020 7416 5222 *website* www.iwm.org.uk) was opened in 2002 and attracts some 6,000 visitors a year to the Department of Printed Books and Documents. Formerly the chapel of the Bethlehem Royal Hospital, or Bedlam, this historic room is used extensively by authors, scholars, journalists and broadcasters. Recently released documents relate, for instance, from 50 boxes of the papers of Field Marshal Bernard Montgomery to the unpublished diaries, letters and memoirs of servicemen and women describing their experiences in both world wars.

Don't forget your local library as the first port of call for any research task. And wherever you are, always follow the researcher's basic code:

1 Know what you need or want
2 Ask the right person or someone who can find the right person
3 Be polite and persistent

Following the above procedure I approached a piece on the national incidence of caesarean section thus:

1 I needed and/or wanted the following information: how many caesarean sections are performed annually? What are the risks? How does it affect the baby? Can any woman not in real medical need choose this method of giving birth? If not, who can – and why do they do so? Is it ever or often regretted?
2 I asked obstetricians and gynaecologists, midwives and the National Childbirth Trust, among others, for professional information. Libraries and statistics resources provided up-to-date facts and figures. Most importantly, I asked women themselves.
3 At all times – particularly on such a personal and sensitive investigation – my polite persistence received helpful, interested and well-informed responses from everyone I met or questioned.

A pleasant bonus occurred as I researched this topic: not only were the people I questioned helpful, they were also keenly anxious, from their various points of view, to aid the spread of information about the whole matter. Go on, they urged me, tell it to the wider world of women. There is so much *mis*-information. While this enthusiasm made my job easier, it also made me realise how essential it is to research well, to get the facts right, and to put it over to a new readership so they understand it too.

Every public library uses the Dewey Decimal system to catalogue books and understanding how it works will save writers time wasted by looking in the wrong place. It works on the following system of classification:

000 Generalities
100 Philosophy & psychology
200 Religion
300 Social sciences
400 Language
500 Natural sciences & mathematics
600 Technology (Applied sciences)
700 The arts
800 Literature & rhetoric
900 Geography & history

In each category lie many subdivisions – for example 304 Factors affecting social behavior, 649 Child-rearing & home care of sick, 386 Inland waterway & ferry transportation. It is easy to become familiar with the system and let it work for you.

Most borrowers and readers who use the reference departments make use of only a small part of what is available to them; further delving into what's on offer could be a welcome eye-opener. New writers may have little idea of what is available until they discover the joys of the local public library. Just set aside a few hours to get to know the way round yours and it could be the most valuable time you've spent in all your research. The library you find most useful may well be the one in your own town but there are plenty of others available.

All major newspapers house their own libraries of press cuttings taken from their pages as it is the task of several employees to snip every separate topic and file it away. Writers have cause to rejoice that they do so, for enquirers to newspaper libraries are (in my experience) generally treated efficiently and courteously. Some may insist that the enquirer be a member of the staff although a commissioned or contributing freelance may be given more consideration than a stranger. If the library staff do not know you, be sure to tell them you are commissioned to write an article for the paper or have been invited to submit one, if that is the case. For some papers a commissioning letter is required before you may make free enquiries; mentioning that the editor or features editor has suggested you contact the library will remove any doubts. Anyone with time-wasting, amateur or unreasonable requests will not be well received. Enquiries should be succinct, clearly stating the date or approximate date of the required cutting or cuttings and when you need the information.

Unfortunately what may still be a free or inexpensive service to those with good contacts is likely to cost unknown beginners hard cash. 'Shall I risk it?' you may ask yourself when faced with the choice of paying for reliable information or making an educated guess. Just remember, your reputation now and in the future might be the price you have to pay.

Other invaluable resources include:

- *The British Library Newspaper Library* (Colindale Avenue, London NW9 5HE *tel* 020 7412 7353 *email* newspaper@)bl.uk *website* www.bl.uk/collections/newspapers.html)
  This is referred to in the trade as simply 'Colindale' and you'll find it in Colindale Avenue in northwest London, almost opposite Colindale Underground Station (Edgware branch of the Northern Line). Opening hours are Monday to Saturday, 10 a.m. to 4.45 p.m. except on public holidays and certain additional days. You can gain admittance if you are over 18 and have a *bona fide* reason for research that involves consulting material not easily available in other libraries. You'll need a Newspaper Library reader's pass which is issued to applicants in person on site. Take a proof of identity document with your signature on it – passport, driving licence or bank cheque card. To get an annual pass you must also provide proof of your address and your need to use the library on a regular basis. If you have a British Library photographic reader's pass you'll be admitted without questions. You are strongly advised to book a place. You can make advance reservations for up to four items by telephoning or emailing the library, preferably 48 hours in advance of your visit.
- *The P A News Centre* (Central Park, New Lane, Leeds LS11 5DZ *tel* 0870 8306824 *email* palibrary@pa.press.net *website* www.pa.press.net)

The library holds more than 14 million news cuttings as well as a photo library housing over 5 million images. Founded in 1868, it is the 24-hour national news agency of the UK and Republic of Ireland and is owned by regional newspaper publishers. Here you may find cuttings dating back to 1928 on every conceivable subject covered from every imaginable angle. There is also a collection of daily events listed for the past five years, 'who said what' quotes for the last year and an outstanding selection of standard reference books. Personal callers are welcome or research may be undertaken on your behalf by in-house staff.

With every cutting, no matter where you find it, check *everything*: the spelling of names and places and all the contents. Do the same (of course) everywhere you go and whenever you collect material from, for instance, officials in police stations, hospitals and other public places. This is particularly important in times of crisis or urgency when facts are so easily – and innocently – incorrectly reported.

The trade itself

People in the newspaper industry and publications about it are helpful to freelances. Here is a selection:

- *The Press Gazette* (formerly the *UK Press Gazette*) (Quantum House, 19 Scarbrook Road, Croydon, Surrey CR9 1LX *tel* 020 8565 4200 *email* pged@qpp.co.uk)
  Weekly for all journalists in regional and national papers (and magazines) carrying news, features and analysis of all areas of journalism.
- *The Author* (The Society of Authors, 84 Drayton Gardens, London SW10 9SB *tel* 020 7373 6642 *email* info@societyofauthors.org *website* www.societyofauthors.org)
  A quarterly magazine sent free to full members and for a fee to non-members.
- *National Union of Journalists* (Headland House, 308 Gray's Inn Road, London WC1X 8DP *tel* 020 7278 7916 *email* info@nuj.org.uk website http://www.nuj.org.uk/front/index.php)

At the time of writing, current membership of one of the biggest and best-established journalists' unions in the world is 34,000 members. The NUJ covers the whole range of editorial work – staff and freelance, writers and reporters, editors and sub-editors, photographers and illustrators, working in broadcasting, newspapers, magazines, books, on the internet and in public relations. There is a London branch solely for freelances while others are attached to branches in other areas of the country. Prospective members have to be proposed and seconded for membership by existing ones. Contact Head Office for information about your nearest branch-meeting. Freelances in all ways receive the same treatment as staff employees on newspapers and magazines. The union publishes a Freelance Directory.

- *The Chartered Institute of Journalists* (2 Dock Offices, Surrey Quays, Lower Road, London SE16 2XU *tel* 020 7252 1187 *email* membershipservices@ioj.co.uk *website* www.ioj.co.uk)
  This organisation was founded in 1884 and has accumulated funds for the assistance of members with legal and other problems.
- *The Society of Women Writers & Journalists* (4 Larch Way, Haywards Heath, West Sussex RH17 5BG *tel* 01444 412087 *email* swwriters@aol.com)
  A society of professional and amateur women writers in every field.

Other help can come from an army of Public Relations folk who are out there just waiting for your queries. PR officers or departments of industries, tourist boards, arts associations, volunteer support groups, political parties, environmental organisations – it sometimes seems the world is only too anxious to give you useful information and it's all free. Contact the promotions or PR departments of associations and organisations relevant to your subject and you may find yourself inundated with material.

I think so-called junk mail was invented for my delight. Everything non-writers might toss in the wastepaper basket with nary a glance I pore over eagerly. Free *useful* information lands on my doormat daily by the see-through wrapper-full, and long may it continue to do so. Do you read yours? I've never directly sought the junk mail that comes my way; I don't have to. But whenever I read 'Tick here if you'd like to be on our mailing list,' I tick.

If you're desperate for help with research, typing, word-processing, photocopying and similar practical tasks you need only look in the pages of writers' publications where researchers, typists, owners of word-processors and folk wanting to edit and improve your work advertise their services. Most are honest people offering to help you and make their livings or add to their incomes at the same time; others are only out to get your money and care nothing about your eventual success. Like you, I have no way of judging – except by personal recommendation from friends and colleagues – which are which.

You are not alone

Writing is a solitary business. When all the guides have been read, the ideas tossed about and the research completed, it remains a matter of sitting down on your own and *writing* – for days, weeks, months, even for years. Meeting others of like mind may be more than an opportunity to get away from the word-processor or typewriter; it may broaden your outlook and strengthen your resolve. Only you can decide what you want. You may find members of writers' organisations and conferences a spur or a bore; helpful or hopeless; not to be missed or to be avoided like rejection slips.

Writers' circles are the starting point for many freelances. Among their members you will find writers of all sorts but one thing you can count on: whatever type of writing they do they will all know the regional or local paper, where budding newspaper writers often count their first successes. I've found every group I've ever visited immensely friendly but only you can judge whether the one you attend is going to be of value to you or whether it is just a talking shop of mutual and meaningless self-congratulation. Most writers' circles number amateurs among their members (who can start as anything else?) but an increasing number include writers published in all *genres* with a high level of achievement. I know many established writers who claim they owe much of their success to the help and encouragement they received from writers' groups and the friends they made as members.

If you would like to join a writers' circle but don't know of one in your district you may find what you want in a handbook that lists them – and offers general help with writing on a variety of topics. The *Writers' Circles Handbook* costs £5 post-free and is available from Oldacre, Horderns Park Road, Chapel-en-le-Frith, High Peak SK23 9SY.

There are many residential and non-residential schools and conferences where writers of all types gather to socialise and learn more of their craft. So numerous are they that I have space to mention only the largest, probably the oldest and certainly the best known. This is the Writers' Summer School held in rural Derbyshire for six days every August. Further details may be acquired from the Secretary, Jean Sutton (10 Stag Road, Lake, Isle of Wight PO36 8PE *tel* 01983 406759 *email* jean.sutton@lineone.net).

More useful resource sites

- The Arts Council of England, 14 Great Peter Street, London SW1P 3NQ *tel* 020 7333 0100 *email* enquiries@artscouncil.org.uk *website* www.artscouncil.org.uk (Scotland and Wales have separate Arts Councils). Regional Arts Associations regularly host lectures and tours by established writers (watch your local or regional press for details) and courses for writers are often organised by WEAs and local authorities.
- *No. 10 Downing Street*: www.number-10.gov.uk (press releases, recent speeches by the Prime Minister, the Queen's Speech, biographies of Cabinet and past PMs and notes on current legislation)
- *Profnet*: http://www3.profnet.com (contacting academic experts using the Committee of Vice-Chancellors and Principals email service)
- *Scottish Parliament*: www.scottish.parliament.uk
- *United Kingdom Parliament*: www.parliament.uk (information about the UK Parliament, House of Commons and House of Lords)
- *Travel Guide*: www.uktravel.com (pix of UK towns and cities, with general information and weather reports)

- *Foreign and Commonwealth Office*: www.fco.gov.uk (the British Government department responsible for overseas relations and foreign affairs)
- *PR Newswire*: www.prnewswire.com (source of immediate news/press releases from corporations worldwide)

The Journalist's Handbook (66 John Finnie Street, Kilmarnock KA1 1BS *tel* 01563 530830 *email* jh@carrickmedia.demon.co.uk) is a reference guide of enormous help in research. Published quarterly, it is free to leading journalists in the UK. You may find it hard to get hold of a copy but keep trying – it is worth it. It contains page after page of sources of information, where you can find any organisation from *The Governing Council of the Cat Fancy*, *Portland College* in Nottinghamshire (a national residential college for people with physical disabilities) and *Morwellham Quay Historic Port and Copper Mine* in Tavistock to *The Raptor Foundation*, a bird of prey sanctuary in Cambridgeshire. There is also a useful *Journalist's Diary* giving details of forthcoming events on which to base your stories, and a guide to the web carrying many pages of invaluable resources of information.

Keeping secrets

When you've done all you can for your piece and made use of every scrap of help you can find and your copy is written, does the research show through? Is it apparent to readers that you've been raiding libraries, filling in facts from reference books and quoting from cuttings that may have already been seen by too many eyes? Always remember that research used well is invisible. Only you will know how long it took you, what hard (but *fascinating*) work it was and how carefully you have rewritten – and *re*written – your copy lest your research has tempted you to write like a learned professor instead of a newspaper freelance. While the world has room and need for both, we journalists know where our feet must always remain: on the ground.

'*If a man is not talented enough to be a novelist, nor smart enough to be a lawyer, and his hands are too shaky to perform operations, he becomes a journalist.*' Norman Mailer

9. The Electronic Writer

The internet has become an essential tool for most writers and everyone who has contributed to the structure and content of the World Wide Web ('the web') can claim a share in its increasing success over the past few years. Whether used for spreading information, promoting a wide assortment of interests for business, sport, or pleasure – even for playing games, making good use of this wonderful new medium can be very helpful and productive for a writer.

It is hard to imagine writing without the benefit of a computer. Yet all the great writers in the past managed it very well indeed. Perhaps it's true to say what you've never had you never miss. To us, word-processing is so easy it can beguile us into imagining our writing ability is rather better than it may be. Terms like 'cut and paste' are no longer mysteries. Even the few of us who still use manual or electric typewriters or the more modern word-processing machines can expect to be asked to submit copy to newspaper editors on floppy disks. (The term 'floppy disk' is a great misnomer: such disks used to be thin and floppy but are now barely flexible in a hard plastic casing.)

Word-processing is a boon to writers, but no sooner had most of us grown used to it than the boffins introduced us to email and the internet – both of which have had a profound effect on the way we work. Whatever sort of writer you may be the internet offers you a huge (often bafflingly so) store of information for research – resources not by the thousand but by the million, and this is no exaggeration. All human knowledge is here, they say, even if some of it only serves to clutter up the writer's mind. To be able to access it is simple enough, but how to discern what is it useful to us and what is not – that's often harder. Imagine being able to open all the pages of the books in a large library at the same time: what confusion. The sooner you learn how to define your search and not get bogged down by excessive irrelevant information, the sooner the internet will be your servant rather than your master.

In some respects the internet is rather haphazard. Nobody actually owns it. Individual pages are created and set up by their authors, and it is on some of these that you will find invaluable if not essential information. Always bear in mind some pages may not be accurate; some may be misleading, or just irrelevant.

Apart from its positive use as a research tool the internet is extremely handy for purely administrative purposes. You can order books, find out what other experts in your field have to say and discover whether anyone else has written any books you might find to be of interest on your chosen topic. All we need to do is sit at home with a computer correctly set up (and it's very simple to do) with the right equipment (which is not expensive now) – and the world is open to us. There are many books about the internet and how to access it: one of the best is *The Internet: A Writer's Guide* by Jane Dorner, published by A & C Black. Some books are written specifically for writers but in this chapter we may only look at the broad principles of what's on offer to us for our benefit and how to make the best use of it.

The internet is not just for providing information, invaluable as that is. Many software packages are there just waiting for you to download into your own computer to help with general and specific writing problems and day-to-day tasks. Some of these programs are free, others allow you to try them for a while (generally a month) before some computer magic tells you you'll have to pay if you want to carry on and yet others demand payment before you even try them. The last are not very common unless they are extremely sophisticated, as most software developers have realised that customers who have a chance to try the goods for nothing are more inclined to buy them than those who are expected to pay out without a clear idea of what the programs will do. (As for just how they make your computer count the free days before telling you they're over – I leave that to the computer wizards.)

Compression files are available on the internet for downloading. These are files such as Win-Zip, which will squash any of your files to take up less room on a disk than they did before compression. Imagine you have completed your copy to send to an editor but fear it will take too long to email to him or for him to bother to read. It may also be taking up too much room on your computer's hard drive and you need to free up some space for other work. Put whatever files you like through Win-Zip and they are instantly (and safely) compressed. There are other compression programs but Win-Zip is the most commonly used and – this is the important bit – an editor or anyone else who receives a Win-Zipped file can only 'unzip' it if he also has Win-Zip. So be sure to find out which compression programme he uses, if any. Although other compression packages might offer more tempting fancy bells and whistles, it is wise to stick to whatever almost everyone has and uses. You can find Win-Zip on www.winzip.com on the internet.

Cheap communication by email

Quick and easy communication by email is one of the most useful time-saving delights of being online and is usually the first experience for new internet users. With great ease we can send text-written messages to fellow writers or to anyone else who has an email address. The message we send (typed on our keyboard and visible on our screens) can appear on recipients' computer screens next-door, at the other side of the country, or in any country anywhere in the world. If the recipient does not have a computer connected at the time, the message will sit there waiting patiently until it *is* connected, when the recipient will immediately be able to download and read it. Furthermore, if you were to send the same message to 20 or to several hundred people you could do so with equal ease.

The action of sending an email message is simplicity itself. Whichever software your computer uses (there are several different programs serving a similar purpose) at the touch of a key a screen will present itself to you, awaiting your message. Just type it, complete the email address(es) of the recipient(s) and click on 'send'. To set your computer up for this operation you will need an Internet Service Provider (commonly referred to as an ISP) which connects you to the system. Most service providers charge a monthly fee but when this has been paid you can send (virtually) as many emails as you like without further expense –

except, of course, the telephone cost of each call. Most leading ISPs run a packaged deal whereby a monthly fee is paid, currently from about £9.99 to £15.99 (plus VAT) and many do not involve you being charged extra on your phone bill while you are online.

Of course email works both ways, and when someone else sends you an email it will appear on your screen. When you have received it you can decide whether to leave it in your in-tray until later, to read it straightaway (and then to keep or delete it) or to act upon it.

Supposing you want to send a file by email – copies of your work to an editor perhaps? Written work, ready to submit to an editor, is easily sent as an email message or as an attachment to an email. So are pictures, known as graphics, and even music (sound files). Follow the instructions provided by your Internet Service Provider and you will find that the attachment you want to send is sent just as that without difficulty. But don't send any files or attachments unless your editor has agreed to accept them: virus infection is a constant worry unless a good virus-detector is employed.

As with instructions on the use of anything, be it a new lawn-mower or a DVD player, reading the manual is less attractive than trying it out for yourself. Most buyers of new gadgets don't read the manual until after they've tried out the product. We want to get our hands on it to see how it works. That is why in learning about the internet and email, if you can find a friend who is already acquainted with it and knows how it works, you will learn so much more than if you sit down and plod through the written instructions. You will soon discover that connection to the internet and confident usage of it is not daunting at all.

Other uses for email spring to mind as soon as you get a taste for it. You can email query letters to editors – if that is how they prefer to be contacted. You can save an enormous amount on postage and stationery and time. Yes, I know you have to pay your ISP – but if you do a lot of communication with fellow writers, research sources etc. you will soon be saving money rather than spending it. If you submit your work to an editor electronically, i.e. online, you will usually get a quicker response than you might have done had you sent it via the old 'snail mail'. You will also be saving yourself (and him) time and money. However far away the recipient editor may be will make no difference; it's just as easy to submit work to a newspaper in the United States as it is to your local paper. And submitting electronically to an editor – anywhere – will go some way towards showing him your professional approach . . . but *only if he expects to receive queries or submissions this way.* Of course there are risks. Not all newspaper editors like to receive copy online and some of those who do may have a greater faith in their staff than is justifiable. It's possible that your copy, carefully edited and submitted online, may spend quite a while languishing on a secretary's machine unseen by anyone else and not passed on any further.

Does email have no disadvantages – cons? (Incidentally, do you know what 'pros' and 'cons' really are? Are they abbreviations for longer words, and if so, what words? As a writer, are you not curious? I will leave the answer to the end of this chapter in case you want to turn to a dictionary and find out for yourself. It is a far more satisfactory way of remembering something than merely reading it when it has been answered by someone else.)

Here is one 'con': invite email from other people and you can get too much, including a lot of rubbish – material you do not want at all. Unsolicited advertising may also come your way. But this is simply deleted and so cannot be counted as too much of a disadvantage. You cannot send email letters to folk if you don't have their email addresses any more than you can post 'snail-mail' letters to people without knowing their postal addresses – if you expect your letters to be received. Fortunately you can find out other people's email addresses: if they are not available for you to ask, yes, you've guessed it, there is a facility for finding them on the web itself.

Sending copy (or anything else) to anyone from your computer is easy – you just press the magic button. Perhaps because it is so simple it is also easy to press it by mistake. So before sending any electronic query or copy to an editor, send it to yourself. This lets you spot any mistakes or transmission problems and deal with them in private. Begin every email message with your name and contact details. If you have already been in contact with an editor or his underling state the nature of your message or the title of your copy. To avoid problems in formatting copy, convert it into plain, single-spaced text format before sending it out as an email message. A 12-point font size is easy to read and the first line of new paragraphs should be indented. Some email programs allow you to add special effects to text.

Naming your files

With so many files to juggle with and create, it is important to name each one wisely for easy reference when you want them again. I make file-naming as plain as I can: 'jones re petunias 16jun02' tells me I was contacting a man named Jones about petunias (which I was writing about at the time) on 16th June 2002. Yes, I know the dates of files are visible in directories but I like to see them in the file name itself, to save the extra step of having to look them up in a directory to find out when I created or last accessed them. So try to give your files and folders names that instantly remind you what they are. The whole purpose of using email and the internet – or even using a computer – is to make it help your writing life.

Using the internet to research, promote and publish your work

Even if you are not a computer buff, you are sure to have heard the phrase 'surfing the net'. You will have realised that the words *net*, *internet*, *web* and *world wide web* all refer to the same thing: they are just terms of jargon that have grown up in the rapidly expanding internet business. In the same way, *surfing* is the word used for what we would normally call browsing. Surfing is very addictive. All it means is that you can look up a particular site (again, *website* is the same as *site*) and find yourself so intrigued with whatever you may find by clicking on enticing links that you get carried away by browsing. How often have you done the same thing in a bookshop or whenever an interesting book comes into your hands?

So you are using the web, perhaps for the first time, to research the topic you want to write about. An email has to come from or go to an email address, typically recognised by the familiar '@' in its middle. Website pages have their own addresses, usually, but not always, prefixed by http://www.

Someone somewhere has designed them, filled them with information and links to other pages, and 'uploaded' them onto the net. A 'page' generally refers to the first page on any site. Think of opening an internet site as opening a magazine at random: whichever page you happen to see first will often lead you to another with the words 'turn to page 5' or 'continued on page 6'. On an internet page a 'turn to' instruction is a word or phrase, or sometimes an icon or a picture, generally underlined, which turns into a little hand when your cursor runs over it. Click on the little hand and you've 'turned the page', i.e. brought up a link to another internet page which then appears on your screen. Although email and browsing web pages for information or interest are two separate ways of using the internet, very often you will find links on web pages automatically lead you to email addresses. 'Click here to contact us', a link may suggest, or perhaps it will just be a little hand over an underlined word or picture that when clicked on will lead you to an email screen.

There are thought to be more than 3 billion sites on the web so it's hardly surprising that some searches take quite a while to complete or cannot bring up any results at all. To make the best use of 'search engines' (special internet helpers such as Google that appear on your screen) use a variety of keywords to refine your search. Whichever search engine you use it can only work on the information you offer it.

Publishing your work

You can publish your own work on the internet in many places on many websites. Many online 'publishers' are anxious to put whatever you send them on screen (for a price) for everyone else to see and read. Just think of it – your article could reach an enormous audience all over the world. *But there is no particular guarantee that anyone will ever read it.* For writers of short stories, for instance, some sites are promoted as literary agents, promising writers their stories will be read by top editors who may (I think the word *may* was never so coyly slipped in elsewhere) ask for more to be published and paid for in the traditional manner. This enticement will not hold such attractions for freelance writers for newspapers who can be quite certain no newspaper editor is *ever* going to seek copy this way. Better for us, by far, is to make our own personal websites at a cost of next to nothing, where *we* decide what they will carry.

Virtual writers

Use of the internet has brought new meaning to the word 'virtual'. We've grown used to thinking of it as indicating 'almost as good as', or 'as nearly so as makes no difference' – but while these paraphrases obtain, in internet-parlance it now has an extended meaning. Online, a *virtual* writers' circle tells us it is not an *actual* gathering of writers talking about and sharing their common interests and helping each other face to face . . . but it is *virtually* so. Once we've got used to the idea that we are only meeting online, such mutual sharing of information, help, markets, tips and general discussion can be enormously valuable. No matter that the people we are 'meeting' may be hundreds of miles away, or even on the other side of the world (and the amazing thing is that we may never learn just *where* they live, unless it is relevant to the topics discussed) a wide diversity of fellow-writers able to communicate in this way makes such a 'meeting' fresher and more intriguing, and opens wider opportunities for mutual benefit than many a local writers' circle in the flesh.

For writers unable to leave their homes, a virtual writers' circle is wonderfully helpful. One or two Internet Service Providers run virtual clubs for their subscribers, offering assistance, information and advice among and between other subscribers. For many years I have made good use of an online 'club', being a customer of their internet service and a member of their virtual community of writers. Online they can (and often do) supply me with help on almost every topic. I want to know where to find a particular quotation – back will come the reply as an email. Non-writing queries receive the same assistance; my computer springs a problem I can't resolve – the answer is supplied at once by a fellow member. Very often the answers I receive are not available elsewhere without calling on expensive specialist help. Look for an Internet Service Provider offering this extra service (for no increased monthly charge). Two popular ones are compuserve.com and cix.co.uk – and there are others.

Finding obscure information – and checking what you find

If you would rather not leave your writing desk when you want to consult a dictionary there is a profusion of dictionary and reference material to read as you are online. (This is a particular enticement for writers who are secretly obsessed with playing with their computers – I plead guilty – and just want to make sure or to check that the online solution given is as good as, or the same as, that given in the good old standby on the bookshelf.) But if you don't have, for instance, a recent copy of a good dictionary or a reference book like *Roget's Thesaurus*, the online versions can be an enormous help. And you can be sure that they are giving you accurate information and guidance.

Even with all the electronic help available it is not always easy to find what you want and to avoid being lumbered with a great deal of information you don't. Internet directories are themselves huge electronic files with hundreds, sometimes thousands, of folders and separate files.

Imagine you are wanting information about the use of Turkish baths early in the 20th century: were they only to be found in specific locations – in spa towns, for instance? Were they open to all, men and women, rich and poor?

Whatever information you are looking for be natural in your choice of words when you use an online search engine. These are programs such as Google (www.google.com) or Ask Jeeves (www.ask.co.uk) – and there are many others. Type in what you want to know. Although websites are written in flowing language search engines are being taught to understand non-technical words in everyday use.

In general always use lowercase but if you are seeking information about the country of China, for instance, start it with a capital C. This will exclude a lot of sites about china tableware – which you do not want. You can narrow your search to avoid being flooded with irrelevant information. The more unusual the words you use in searching, the more specific the results will be. Think of valid but uncommon words before you begin; 'car' will return 53,000,000 results, 'toyota' reduces it to under six million but the search narrows down to 359,000 when you enter 'camry'. Be sure to spell your search keywords properly and be aware of differences between English and American spelling, In the case of 'colour' for example, use 'colour OR color'. Some search engines, like Ask Jeeves, will check your spelling for you.

Use Boolean definers (named after mathematician George Boole 1815–1864). They are a system of logical combinations, using words like AND, OR & NOT. It is best to capitalise them.

AND or '+' requires the word to be present: John AND Mary AND Frank *or* John + Mary + Frank
OR allows either word to be present: Peter OR Simon
NOT or '-' excludes words: Marx NOT Brothers or Marx-brothers

Try using reverse questions. Search engines look for pieces of text matching your query but web pages are more likely to contain answers than questions – so search for the answer. Phrase your query as you would expect the answer to read; this may seem a small change but it makes a huge difference. Type 'man first landed on the moon in' rather than 'when did man first land on the moon?'. Note: Ask Jeeves is the exception and comes up with excellent answers to common natural language questions.

Publicity and self-promotion on your own website

The size and rapid growth of the World Wide Web can be largely attributed to the contributions of individuals keen to use the internet to publish information about their individual interests and efforts, in business or pleasure. Using the internet as a self-publicity tool is valuable for freelances. Setting up your own website is itself likely to generate income, if you make a good job of it.

Establishing your presence on the internet is not as difficult as you might imagine. It is not expensive but it does take time and patience to do it well. Setting up your own page involves using a special language called HTML. This stands for a 'hypertext mark-up language' but neither it nor its name need bother us at all. There are many good software programs that make it easy for us to set up our own web pages in simple terms without knowing anything about any special language or specialist terms. *Frontpage*, *Pagemill* and *Dreamweaver* are three that make the job easy – and there are many others. Don't make the page so big that your readers have to scroll up and down to read it – and just as a wodge of solid text deters readers of the printed page, so does it when on the screen. Break your text up into small pieces that are easy to read with plenty of graphics (not too large) and links to other pages or even parts of the same page, for ease of navigation. Make the design of each page reasonably similar to the earlier ones: over-design just for the sake of it is a mistake and only detracts from what the page is trying to say.

To publish your home page on the internet you will need an FTP. That is a 'file transfer program' – a software program that moves your completed web pages from your computer onto the internet where it may be read and seen by other internet users everywhere. Any good web-authoring program makes it easy with step-by-step instructions.

Setting up your own web page is akin to writing your CV online so that everyone and anyone who cares to access it can see it. You could also provide links to other pages featuring books you have published, or work you have written and not yet published. In this way you can sell yourself to editors with details of your published credits in the world of writing. Although having your own web page can be profitable it does not replace any of the self-publicity you could and should be doing elsewhere. There are still many thousands or millions of people who even in this technological age do not or cannot access the internet.

Once you have set up your web page you will of course want people to visit – there is no point in having one otherwise. So you must advertise it just as you advertise yourself on your letterheads. On your web page put links to other writers of interest that you find on other sites and ask them, in return, to put your page as a link on their sites. Contact the various search engine operators so that they will put you on their lists (although you will generally have to pay for this) and folk browsing the net searching for writers in your specialised field will find your site. A successful site will make its own mark and should be updated frequently. Even if you haven't anything new to add to it apart from some new links, a change of layout or typeface will help keep it looking fresh and inviting.

Is there money in it?

The line between having your work published online and vanity-publishing is a thin one. You see an editor asking for submissions; you send your copy online, to appear in his online publication. What, exactly, have you agreed to let him have? Online publication is a gift for vanity publishers. The technicalities of accepting your copy are quick, easy and cost very little. Before you know it, what you have innocently sent may be appearing in an e-book or be distributed to places and readers unknown to you – *at no profit at all to you*. Proceed with great caution. Once such online publishers have your copy, why should they bother to sell or promote it for you? 'Let us put it online for you,' they may offer, 'and editors all over the country – and the world – will read your work, appreciate how well you can write *and want to pay for your copy*.' Really? I am not denying this has happened but if there are such editors they hide themselves away well. Openings for writers to submit online copy to be published in online versions of newspapers are (understandably) rare. Of more help to us, online, are the many sites of help, advice and marketing guidance referred to above.

Websites to target

There are dozens of websites covering the world of writing and more arrive on your screens almost every day. Some are of flimsy value to writers but others deserve investigation. Here are some to try. Although not all directed at writing for and selling to newspapers they are pointers to greater learning and understanding of the magazine and newspaper publishing industry here and overseas.

- www.publist.com (no, not a list of public houses but general help for writers including a classified section on who is buying what in the world of periodicals)
- www.journalism.co.uk (published by an online publishing company in Brighton, carrying useful links to national, regional and local newspapers and news sources)

- www.writersdigest.com (a major US site for writers. *Writer's Digest* is the world's leading magazine for writers, founded in 1920. Bound to be useful for all writers everywhere in every genre)
- www.4journalism.com (another US site with fascinating links to the history of (US) newspapers, famous newspaper hoaxes and much more)
- www.forwriters.com (another American site, describing itself thus: *this site is for those who have been forced by their own muse into the wonder, frustration, pain and joy of this wonderful art form*)

Copyright on the net

United Kingdom law decrees that material published on the internet is protected by copyright but the ease with which it can be copied by almost anyone puts it in a vulnerable position. Under the Berne Convention to which most leading nations subscribe, as soon as writing is put into 'tangible' form – i.e. as soon as it exists – it is protected by copyright . . . and work on the internet falls into this classification. A European directive also makes it clear that authors are entitled to control and be remunerated for any electronic use made of their work.

Inevitably, with the scope of the internet being so enormous, you are very unlikely to discover if/when anyone 'pirates' your copy. If you do find trouble these sites may prove helpful:

- www.alcs.co.uk (the Authors' Licensing & Collecting Society, established in 1997 to help protect our rights – and use them to the full. It distributes fees to writers whose work has been copied, broadcast or recorded)
- www.benedict.com (an American site telling you all you need to know about internet copyright and its infringement)

If the wonders of electronic gadgetry amaze and intrigue us, commonplace as it is in today's workaday environment, we are told what we use now is nothing to the marvels ahead. Maybe they are not so far ahead either, for research and development are rapid. Leeds University engineers are now working on highly sensitive 'terahertz waves' which may enable us to 'see' the writing on pages of a book – without opening it. Hmm. That might not please everyone who reads for pleasure: rather like eating a meal without being able to taste or see it. But for other 'reading' purposes, such as rapid research . . .

(*Pro* is latin for *in favour* and is not abbreviated. *Con* is an abbreviation of *contra*, meaning *against*.)

10. Business

Adopting a businesslike attitude does not sully the art of writing, as some folk claim. The truth is that if you mean business you have to be both a writer and a record-keeper. Because I want to be a professional writer more than I want to be a record-keeper I long ago devised a system that a) demands little time, b) keeps my affairs in order, and c) satisfies the Inland Revenue. That is why I urge you to study this chapter closely; not necessarily to model your own system on mine, but to appreciate the value of getting the 'business' straight from the beginning. You won't regret it.

Don't misunderstand the word 'professional' in talking about your writing. Regardless of whether you do a little or a lot, write daily, weekly or just occasionally, being professional is an attitude of mind; you can be just as professional when you only write a couple of articles a year as when you are filing copy every day to a top national newspaper. Countless 'occasional' writers want no other status and would certainly not wish to be caught up in what they see as a deal of paperwork and business hassle, especially if they have just retired from a lifetime of it. As for the quality of the finished product – the written word – that is what counts.

Being businesslike is itself good business. Working with your affairs and papers in a muddle will make life harder because you may not be able to find essential letters, agreements, disks and other references when you want them, with the resultant mistakes and missed opportunities such confusion may generate; it will also give other people the impression that you are not likely to do a good job of work with your writing when you're in a state of constant chaos. Getting straight in your mind as well as on your desk is not just a matter of personal satisfaction but one of practical importance. Being methodical about your records will increase your confidence and free you from worry.

Tax facts

Whatever you are paid should be gross, not net. Freelances are self-employed and registration with your tax authority in this capacity should ensure you are paid without deductions. It also lets you claim a range of expenses to be set against any tax you may have to pay, before the tax is calculated. The task of self-assessment was imposed on all writers (and other folk) classed as self-employed in April 1997. In general terms, it involves the taxpayer calculating the tax payable on income, rather than leaving it to the Inland Revenue.

When you earn money for your work, be it ever so little, the Inland Revenue will want to know. It's a mistake to think, 'Some small cheques for articles I sold to X newspaper – that isn't worth bothering about.' Alas, it is. Not only because there might be some awkward questions from the tax inspector when you become better known but also because of those expenses you can set against any tax you might have to pay on your earnings. There are significant variations in tax law concerning employed and self-employed writers so it will certainly help to behave at all times as the self-employed writer you are. Use private headed stationery and work on your own equipment. Make sure you are paid on the basis of work done, not hours worked. Make your own arrangements for insurance, pensions and so on, and (probably the best safeguard against taxation at source) do not work exclusively for one market. It could be hard to convince the Inland Revenue of your freelance status unless you work, or have worked, for at least three or four different employers in the course of a single tax year.

Self-assessment of tax involves submitting tax returns on specific dates. If you want the Inland Revenue to calculate your tax for you they must receive your information by the end of September, or by the end of January the following year if you or your accountant have worked out the tax payable. As a freelance you pay tax on the income you expect to earn in the current tax year.

From past knowledge of our tax affairs the Inland Revenue sends (or should send) each of us only the appropriate pages to complete but it remains our responsibility to see that we receive them. All income from writing must be declared, as must income from other sources. We have to declare everything on the tax return but do not have to send accounts. There are many specialist firms (and a few sharks) who will do the work for you if you can't or don't fancy doing it. Banks also offer the same service for a fixed fee; 'tax shops' will need to know full details of your affairs and may charge anything up to several hundred pounds, competing with accountants for the work. If you decide to patronise a tax shop, check it carries professional indemnity insurance covering incorrect advice or negligence. Remember that you will be held entirely responsible for errors and mistakes, no matter who actually completed the forms or who advised you in doing so. True to its stony-faced image, the Inland Revenue even makes you pay for the stamp to return your self-assessment forms when you've completed them; even prisoners don't have to pay for their handcuffs. Probably the wisest course of action, if you are not planning on doing-it-yourself, is to seek help from a qualified accountant, preferably a member of the *Chartered Institute of Taxation or the Association of Tax Technicians* (*see* page 163). Whatever you decide, invest in a good tax guide. One of the best for writers is *Lloyds TSB Tax Guide* by Sara Williams & Jonquil Lowe (Penguin Books: £8.99). The Inland Revenue produces various booklets helpful in completing self-assessment forms, details of which may be found on their website http://www.inland revenue.gov.uk/leaflets.

Like everyone else, writers with incomes from writing currently greater than £55,000 per year must register as payers of Value Added Tax with HM Customs & Excise. Those earning less than this figure may also register, at the discretion of Customs & Excise, and you may find it to your benefit to do so. Your local Customs & Excise office will advise you.

Expenses

Against all this gloomy talk of paying tax, you will be able to claim expenses incurred before you actually earn anything at all, providing you tell the Inland Revenue from the beginning that you are in business as a writer. Postage, stationery, telephone calls, printing headed paper and business cards, insurance (if taken out specially) and maintenance of equipment such as your word-processor, tapes, disks, books of reference (including this one), travelling expenses, hotels, meals eaten out in the course of work, secretarial expenses, professional subscriptions – once you start noting your expenses you'll be amazed how they add up. You may also amortize the original cost of whatever equipment you need, a word-processor (a computer may be harder to justify as it does so much more than just write, but you may be lucky), voice-recorder or any other major purchase. Do this by claiming a percentage (usually subject to the capital cost and by negotiation with the tax inspector) of the price paid in the first and subsequent years until the whole sum has been defrayed. Keeping your capital expenses in proportion to your anticipated income is only sensible, particularly at the beginning of your dealings with the Inland Revenue.

Always keep whatever receipts, invitations, details of meetings, travel tickets and even diaries that come your way to produce for the taxman if he wants to see them; it's improbable that he will, but he might. Everything that serves to demonstrate your status as an established freelance is worth saving. Are you attending a writers' conference or school to further your knowledge and experience? Claim those fees, of course – and the cost of getting there and back. Mileage allowances vary greatly and you may be able to discover the rates your target market will pay and reach agreement that such expenses will refunded. Otherwise you should put in a claim at a 'reasonable' rate – see the NUJ's and Society of Authors' most recently published guides. It may be hard to convince the Inland Revenue when you come to claiming for car maintenance and depreciation as these vary even more depending on the model, age and mileage of your car.

Assuming you work in a room in your house specially set aside for the purpose you may legitimately claim for the light, heating and cleaning, plus whatever proportion of rent (if any) it represents in relation to what you pay. You should also be aware that although exemption from Capital Gains Tax applies to your house (or your main house if you own more than one) it does not apply to whatever part of it you use for carrying on a business. This means that if and when you sell the house you will have to pay Capital Gains Tax on that portion of it deemed to be used for your business. This penalty only applies to exclusive use of a room (or rooms) for your work and tax is payable at your highest income rate. It is quite legitimate to claim that the room where you write is not exclusively a work room if you use it for domestic purposes as well, even if only occasionally.

Anyone is free to work from home, but you may need planning permission if you want to build a special extension as a workplace. If you have a mortgage you should tell your lender what you plan to do, if your home is rented check with your landlord first and if you live in council premises let the housing officer know.

Good record-keeping is essential. With it you needn't fear the shadow of the Inland Revenue, while also being fair to yourself.

Training

However you wish to start you must be literate and numerate, be able to write, be eager to learn, be aware of and interested in current affairs, hate boredom and – above all – be fascinated by people, what they do and why. Can you also be accurate about gathering and presenting facts and work to a deadline? Having your feet on the ground (and being able to keep them there) while keeping your wits about you and your head held high are equally essential attributes.

Most (but not all) entrants to training courses are young and what are called 'media studies' are viewed with some scepticism among professional journalists of the 'old' school. Running the local student's paper, the rock band's weekly news-sheet or writing regular support letters for the football team may seem far from what you will later be thinking of as 'journalism' but all such occupations present young writers with a chance to see if they have (or can learn to acquire) the essential basic tools that will serve them all their working lives – the craft of putting words clearly on paper, saying what they mean them to say, in the right order, at the right time and in the right way for the people who are going to read them.

The National Council for the Training of Journalists (NCTJ) organises between 25and 30 training colleges throughout the UK, attracting 600 or more students annually. Double that number train while they work on newspapers and this method probably produces better final results. This being so – and offering the chance to earn a living while working – places offered by the major newspaper groups on their in-house training schemes are hard to win and greatly prized. National and regional groups may offer this chance to youngsters but not many places are available. After 18 months or two years as a junior reporter you must pass the NCTJ certificate of proficiency to get your foot on the next rung of the ladder.

On a local paper you will learn what may appear to be small skills but these will be invaluable to your future career: how to write funeral reports, keep lists of wedding guests, submit inquest verdicts, take notes on proceedings at council meetings, interpret court reports accurately, with many more apparently mundane daily tasks, all to precise deadlines. Working to a deadline is more than a challenge: it is positively beneficial. Without a deadline by which material is to be completed, work tends to drift between stages of rewriting, beginning again and rewriting: a permanent state of metamorphosis in which nothing worthwhile is completed. Looming deadlines cure all that. Early training includes relevant aspects of law: contempt, libel, privilege and the complexities of the Official Secrets Act. Do you know what libel is? Most of us think we do, and when asked would say libel is written and slander is spoken, both being the offence of writing or saying scurrilous or untrue statements about someone else. That is only half the correct answer and it's this distinction between thinking we know and *really* knowing that is so important. A guide issued by the Society of Authors quotes thus: *A libel is a defamatory statement about an identifiable living person or a company still trading. 'Defamatory' means likely to expose a person to hatred, ridicule or contempt.* For journalists a simple definition is this: *Libel exists when someone's character or livelihood is damaged by statements in a paper.* That the allegations are true may not be adequate defence, nor that the story was published in good faith and without malice or understanding. So be careful. The legal meaning of 'Contempt of Court' is also taught but this probably concerns editors and reporters more than freelance writers. Dead people cannot be libelled, although proceedings may be brought by descendants if there has been a suggestion that the deceased suffered from an inheritable mental disease.

The Official Secrets Act was passed in 1989 to replace its predecessor of 1911. It makes it an offence for anyone working for the Crown to disclose, by word of mouth or in writing, information acquired as a result of employment. This restriction applies equally to civil servants, diplomats, soldiers, policemen, members of the judiciary and even Crown gardeners, cleaners, porters and secretaries. The Act was clarified many years ago to cover matters calling for special secrecy for reasons of national security, and it covered the press. These were known as D Notices which were, in effect, government bans on editorial publication of specific items.

You may agree with Lord Northcliffe (the creator of modern popular journalism, who founded the *Daily Mail* in 1896 and originated the picture paper with the *Daily Mirror* in 1903) when he said '*The only way to teach people to write is to have them write*,' and there is no doubt this basic start to a career has proved a grounding many now established journalists vow gave them their greatest strength. Former *Daily Mail* editor David English said, '*Journalism is a skill that can only be acquired on the job and at the end of the day it depends on whether someone has a burning individual talent.*' Many years later television presenter Jon Snow told a conference organised for student journalists: '*It's a fantastic time to become a hack. There is a new realisation dawning that the people who will have to explain this new world order – or disorder – will be people who have an understanding of what's going on. Information and journalism can never be second-hand. Eyewitness is the key. We are, as journalists, the eyes and ears of people who cannot attend the event themselves.*'

University and college courses

Graduate entry is now commonplace. The first degree does not necessarily have to be in a subject related to journalism. It is generally recognised that a postgraduate journalism course encapsulates the best training of all. Many if not most of our leading figures in the industry found their way up the ladder by this route which now accounts for about half the entrants to the profession. A vocational course will teach you basic skills: shorthand to the level of at least 100 words a minute, knowledge of the law relevant to journalism, the structure of local and central government and how to write news and features.

From Barnsley College, offering a Higher National Diploma Media course in journalism and a BA (Hons) course in Combined Studies (journalism) to Bournemouth Media School's (at Bournemouth University) full-time, three-year BA (Hons) and BA Hons Multi Media Journalism courses, such opportunity for study is available at centres up and down the country. Multi-Media Journalism is a very demanding course which produces graduates able to compete for jobs in newspapers, magazines, broadcasting and online journalism. All Bournemouth's staff teaching professional skills are practising or former senior journalists. The course seeks to deliver those skills. It is the only course in the UK accredited by all three leading industry training bodies: the Broadcast Journalism Training Council, the National Council for the Training of Journalists and the Periodicals Training Council. Following these courses, graduate employment rate is currently 83%.

Other ways into the job include privately run 'training' courses (my quotation marks reveal my caution about their frequent claims for outstanding success and lofty salaries after paying their high fees), learning from correspondence or internet courses run by – well, you don't always see the credentials of the tutors – and daytime and evening courses, barely stimulating or excellent by the luck of the draw, run by local councils or private individuals. '*Information overload*,' puffed one elderly journalist on seeing the range of writing courses available. '*Just get out there and write*.'

You may find some writers who have benefitted from taking a correspondence course and I cannot deny they may be helpful to beginners or those just wanting some guidance on occasional submissions to editors. But they are an expensive way of learning what can be discovered more quickly and easily from reading a book like this one at a fraction of the cost. The late John Diamond revealed in the *Spectator* that one correspondence college was, in the new 21st century, still talking about typewriters and copy paper and blacks and hot metal – practices that died out with the arrival of mass computerisation decades ago. If you want to make writing for newspapers earn you good money, don't waste it on correspondence courses whose tutors may be only experienced in running correspondence courses. If their expertise lies in journalism itself, which pays a great deal better, why are they running courses by post?

More official routes involve National Vocational Qualifications (NVQs) run by the Newspaper Society, two-year HNDs and The London School of Journalism's course. The latter covers home-study in all areas of news journalism, freelance and feature writing. It also offers three and six-month postgraduate diploma courses in journalism in London which are recognised by the National Union of Journalists, and an intensive course in journalism and newswriting at an annual Summer School.

At any age you can 'do-it-yourself'. Whatever your degree status or scholastic achievements and whichever way you approach your career, an approved apprenticeship must be served. To make the very best of it you will, at least, have an abiding curiosity, an awareness of logic and order, and a love of words. Without these, training or not, you are a non-starter.

The cost of vanity

Ask any writer. There is nothing quite like the joy of seeing – for the first time – your work published in a newspaper. Even after dozens of successes full-time professionals never forget that wondrous internal delight: it's there in print, it has your name on it, and you are being paid for it.

But what if you can't get to that stage? Supposing – and it happens to many thousands of writers – you have worked as hard as you can, cut, pruned, polished and laboured over your baby until you can do no more, and yet still no editor wants it. It can be a wearisome and very lengthy task, as so many of us know. Yet you cannot give up. The passion for publication just will not go away. Your work deserves it, you tell yourself. Surely somebody, somewhere . . .

One day you find the solution. 'Writers wanted' you read, perhaps in a magazine or newspaper especially for writers. While such enticements are generally aimed at and appeal to writers of books more than freelance articles, anyone in the business of what we call 'vanity publishing' is not fussy about who his customers might be. He is probably a 'publisher' who, far from accepting that he must pay his contributors for their work, expects you to give him yours for nothing. Sometimes, particularly in the case of books or small-press newspapers and magazines, he will also ask you to pay him for the 'privilege' of seeing it in print. This is a worse position than writing for established editors who are reluctant to pay you, for at least they may negotiate and reach a sensible paying solution. Not so Mr Vanity Publisher; all he wants is your work *free*.

Since his prime purpose is to take your money by trading on the vanity all we writers are prey to, he will be quite busy: there are plenty of other writers in the same can't-get-published position. But he won't be too busy to accept whatever you send him. Frankly, the quality of it and your ability as a writer are not of great importance to him; all he needs to run a successful business is eager clients. He won't want to change or edit what you have written either, for that takes time and effort. He prefers to print it more or less (or even exactly) as you sent it to him, warts and all. There in cold print will be all your typing errors, grammatical mistakes and every misjudgement of the brain and finger. If Mr VP is putting together a small booklet or newspaper (and do not misunderstand me; there are many such publications of integrity and worth) when you have given him your work for nothing the only way you can see it in print may be to buy his publication, perhaps having to agree to paying a regular subscription for several months or a year. You are, in effect, paying him for what you have already given him. There will be profit from the sale of his publication because – alas – other folk will be happy to buy it to see their work in print. Of course all the profit from sales goes into his pocket. It's sad but true: once Mr VP has your money his only wish is for you to go away and not bother him any more. Further information about the perils and evils of vanity publishing are obtainable from Johnathon Clifford, 27 Mill Road, Fareham, Hampshire PO16 0TH *tel* 01329 822218 *email* johnathonclifford@compuserve.com

In recent years, through voluntary advice and campaigning, Johnathon Clifford has saved or retrieved millions of pounds for authors worldwide and has been instrumental in the issuing of warrants for the arrest of nine of the worst vanity publishers for fraud. This is one of the invaluable warnings he offers to careful writers, in this case about Hamilton & Co Publishing Ltd and Central Publishing Ltd:

Mal Sykes has been writing to authors expressing his 'personal apologies' for the fact that Hamilton are in the process of going into liquidation, and offering – for a fee – to take over the publication of books that were to be published by Hamilton by the new company – Central Publishing Ltd, – he has set up as a result of his 'being unhappy with the level of service offered by Hamilton'. He also states that 'We were all made redundant last Friday.' What he fails to tell authors is that according to Companies House on 29 March 2001, Malcolm Peter Sykes is the sole Director of Hamilton & Co and also the sole Director of Central Publishing Ltd.'

Never fall into the hands of Mr Vanity Publisher and his ilk. Quite apart from the burdensome disappointment, you risk damaging your reputation for the day when your work is published through the accepted commercial channels. In professional circles vanity publishing is considered the last resort of the desperate. It will gain you no respect if you're serious about your writing.

Jargon

Since you began reading this book you have heard a lot of 'in-language'. All occupations have their own, much of it originating long ago and referring to working practices now out of date. It is not surprising that by the very nature of their business, those whose work is words enjoy a particularly rich store of jargon. Here is some that will soon be familiar to you:

Agency copy – material coming from a major news agency such as Reuters, Associated Press or the Press Association
Ampersand (&) – the typographical sign for 'and'
Backgrounder – a story enlarging on the main story of the day
Banner – the main headline across the top of the page
Blink – the act of connecting to networking communication
Body type – the size of type used for most of the paper
Bold – thick dark type used for emphasis
Broadsheet or heavy – large-size paper like the *Daily Telegraph* as opposed to a tabloid/red-top like the *Sun*
Byline – a writer's name at the head or foot of a story

Caps – capital letters used on their own
Cast-off – ending a story, generally in a given space
Catchline – an identifying phrase/word at the top of a page
Copy – editorial material
Copy-taster – the staff person assigned the task of assessing copy
Crosshead or shoulder – a sub-heading, often in bold type, to enliven text
Doorstepping – waiting outside people's front doors for a story
Ear – the advertising space beside a front page title-line
Edition – a one-time print (perhaps with regional variations)
Embargo – the ban on a pre-released story until publication
Email – electronic (internet) mail
File – to submit copy for publication
Freebie – a gift or privilege from a reader/advertiser
Fudge box – space for late news. Also an item in a ruled box
Hard copy – editorial material on paper
House style – spelling, punctuation etc. as the paper likes it
Intro – the opening paragraph
Issue – all copies and editions printed in one day
Layout – sheet ruled into columns showing where copy will go
Lead – the main news story in the paper
Lift – to pass off someone else's work as your own
Literal – a printing error in spelling ect. (*sic*)
Lowercase – small (not capital) letters
Masthead – heading on editorial page giving details of paper
Mid-market – paper falling between heavies and red-tops
Online/offline – connected or not connected to the internet
Par – a paragraph
Pic (plural pix) – abbreviation for photograph(s)
Point – a standard unit of type size; also means a full-stop
Proofs – the first print for checking before the final print
Run on – where a story is not to be broken into pars
Slush – a pile of unsolicited and often unwanted copy
Spike – an imaginary or actual spike for rejected copy
Standfirst (or 'sell') – an intro separate from the story itself
stet – Latin for 'let it stand'
Story – a written item or piece of work
Streamer – a page lead printed across several columns
Stringer – writer (usually overseas) always ready to file copy
Splash – a page one lead story

Strap – a subsidiary headline above a main headline
Shorts – small stories for fillers or down-page items
Subeditor (sub) – a copy editor, headline writer, layout man/woman etc.
Tag – the small type line after the main headline
Tear sheet – a page carrying published copy
Uppercase – capital letters when beside lowercase letters (*see* caps)

Rights – & wrongs

As a self-employed freelance the copyright of everything you write is yours unless you voluntarily give it away, which I hope you never will. Retain your copyright and you can sell your work over and over again. So keeping ownership of your property is more than a matter of principle. It makes no difference whether you submit your copy 'on spec' i.e. without any prior contact with a newspaper or whether an editor asks to see it and even firmly commissions it. It is your intellectual property and you own all rights in it. If you part with them unnecessarily, you are only robbing yourself.

Watch out for alternative terms such as 'assigning rights', which really means handing over copyright itself – but faced with a demand from an editor that you part with copyright, consider offering leased or timed rights. That means you will allow the paper to use your copy exclusively for a given period of time, after which all rights will revert to you. These 'First British Serial Rights' mean you grant the newspaper exclusive use of your material for an agreed few days or a week and this is where careful and informed negotiation can pay dividends.

FBSR is often thought to consign first publication rights for all time, leaving only second or subsidiary rights – but this is not necessarily so. Many editors will want to use your copy only once. A few may take advantage by assuming electronic, overseas and other rights without reference or payment to the freelance. All the more reason to make sure commissions, contracts and business arrangements are satisfactory and as water-tight as you can make them. If you do not state or discuss the rights you are offering your silence may be taken as consent to something you don't want, when it is too late to put the matter straight. A test case in September 1999 upheld the US Court of Appeal's unanimous verdict that the *New York Times* and other titles had infringed freelance writers' copyright by reselling newspaper articles without obtaining the writers' permission or making extra payment to them.

The Universal Declaration of Human Rights (Article 27) emphasises that everyone has the right to the protection of the moral and material interests resulting from any scientific, literary or artistic production of which he/she is the author; and according to the 1988 Copyright Designs and Patent Act, any assignment of copyright, i.e. the ownership of copyright changing hands, has to be confirmed in writing. So it certainly will not do for any editor or publisher to assume you have handed over copyright because it was not specifically mentioned or it was taken for granted that you were willing to part with it.

In truth a better word when talking of selling copyright or handing it over, would be 'licensing' – for all you are doing is renting it out to a particular editor for a designated period. In most cases all publishers may really want is the assurance that copy they buy from you is not being published and will not be published in a competing paper. To keep out of trouble and avoid problems about rights of any sort, just give each paper the rights it needs and don't innocently lose more than you need.

This is the wording suggested by the NUJ's retained solicitors, for freelances to use when supplying copy to a publisher:

> *I hereby licence X newspaper for a once-off publication on the enclosed copy in its daily/weekly/other newspaper. The licence to publish is subject to payment of the agreed licence fee of X within [specify period]. Copyright in the work remains with me, its author. The work is not permitted to be syndicated, included in a database, published on the internet or otherwise used in any other publication or for any electronic publication. The right of the author to be identified as the author of the work is asserted.*

It's good news that since the adoption of the Copyright Act of 1998 authors and writers for broadcasting and electronic publishing also own another set of rights: moral rights. These are your rights to be identified as the author of the copy, and the right not to have your copy mutilated to your disrepute or edited to reflect anything hurting your honour or reputation. The bad news is that such moral rights were not – and still are not – extended to cover newspapers or magazines.

UK law clearly grants self-employed writers copyright in their copy but a few years ago many freelances received unexpected letters from one of the UK's largest publishing houses for whom they regularly worked. The letters demanded all rights in everything they wrote, loftily assuming world-wide exclusivity for all current and future rights without any further payment.

Other publishers quickly followed suit in the great attempt at copyright grabbing leaving freelances everywhere in a turmoil. What should be done? Most of the writers concerned were full-time professional freelances dependent on their contracts of employment for the bread on their table. Some agreed to losing their rights, not knowing what else to do, but others – in increasing numbers as time passed – stood and fought. It's taking a long time and some progress has been made. But the battle is not yet won; regional titles in Cardiff and Newcastle owned by the Trinity Mirror group, the *Mail on Sunday* and several more papers are still trying to talk to innocent (and experienced) freelances about all-rights assignments. How many more freelances are being pressured to do the same? You must be aware of what is going on if you are not to fall into the trap of throwing away, or at least selling, that most valuable right of all – copyright.

Apart from the time and trouble it takes to look after your rights, it's a great shame that writers and editors, the people who need their words, so often fail to agree on what is right and fair to everyone. It's all in the name of 'business'. See the *Copyright Licensing Agency*, 90 Tottenham Court Road, London W1T 4LP *tel* 0207 631 5555 *email* cla@cla.co.uk *website* www.cla.co.uk and the *Authors' Licensing and Collecting Society*, Marlborough Court, 14–18 Holborn, London EC1N 2LE *tel* 020 7395 0600 *email* alcs@alcs.co.uk *website* www.alcs.co.uk.

Working for national papers I have several times had cheerful letters or calls from friends on the other side of the world who enjoyed reading the same management's publications in their countries. 'Loved your piece in the paper today,' they would say, not knowing what a surprise the news was to me that anything of mine had been printed over there at the time. Colleagues in the

UK often have the same experience: yes, without any reference or acknowledgement to us, and certainly without any extra payment, our copy (sold for single use here) was being lifted by unscrupulous editors and conglomerates for 'free' use elsewhere.

Alas, it happened then and it is still happening.

Plagiarism

Stealing copy from someone else – taking work written by another writer and pretending you wrote it yourself – is plagiarism. But don't imagine all the baddies are struggling freelance writers trying to earn some money (not that that excuses it, of course). Plagiarism cuts both ways as we've seen above. *The Sun* was the thief when it 'lifted' and printed 800 words of a freelance interview with pop-star Noel Gallagher originally published in a leading music magazine. The freelance took the paper to court, claiming £3,000. Only after months of hassle, and on the day before the court hearing was due, did the litigants agree on a compensatory fee of £2,500. There are many similar cases of newspapers taking freelance copy in print elsewhere and then re-selling the stolen goods. A few are caught and made to pay, literally. How many others are not caught and just get away with theft we shall never know.

Oh yes, we all know the cunning dodges plagiarists get up to: altering a word or phrase here and transposing paragraphs there. No matter what you call it or how you do it, it is common theft. But how are we to judge to what extent other writers have stolen our copy? Could they just have read it, absorbed its content and then written something on the same topic themselves – a subconscious paraphrase? – without any conscious attempt at direct or even indirect 'copying'?

Compare the pieces opposite. The one on the left is my copy, as published in one of my earlier books about writing for newspapers: on the right is a piece taken from a book by an Irish author.

Electronic rights

With the rapid growth of media technology, global companies and the web of cross-media ownership, plagiarism is even more

This is a good place to remind you that stubborn determination to use every scrap of research material you have unearthed, relevant or not, can ruin a good feature. Don't feel you've been working to no purpose and wasting your time if you can't or don't use it all. In any case, you will (I hope) keep everything you've found. Its value in the future will more than reward you for any restraint this first article might impose on you. Never content yourself with writing just one or two pieces about a topic when your research may well keep you funded to sell to local papers, freesheets, regional, trade and maybe daily papers as well. I confess the only hardship I find in wringing research dry is that I get tired of the subject.	At this point it must be said that stubborn determination to use every scrap of research material you have unearthed, relevant or not, can ruin a good feature. What you leave out is an important as what you include, it won't be wasted. Keep it. Its value in the future, if used properly, will more than reward your restraint. Never be content with writing just one or two pieces about a topic when your research will keep you funded to sell different angles on your subject to different papers, trade, specialist, magazines and overseas. The main problem, as you'll discover in wringing research dry, is that you'll get tired of the subject, be delighted to see the back of it and move on to pastures new.

of a problem. There is barely an attempt to hide it. In 1999 the *Independent* admitted: 'It is common knowledge among freelance journalists that newspapers use the material they write for both written and electronic publication and that the freelance journalist grants us these rights.' At this time no such agreements had been made. A paper's calm assumption that it is buying electronic rights when only text rights have been mentioned is all too common, and takes many freelances unawares. When you negotiate your original agreement and terms, be sure you claim an extra payment for any electronic rights the paper wants to buy.

What will you earn?

Payment to contributors varies widely not only according to what you write or how well you write it but also to who you are. Top-name writers with wide experience and pulling-power can almost demand what they like; an annual income of several hundred thousand pounds is not unknown at this level. Coming down to ours, a freelance contributor to say, the women's or gardening page might be offered up to £30 for the page. Somewhere between those extremes lie most working journalists and many hard-working freelances fare better than staff employees.

A disillusioned Lincolnshire staffer (well-qualified with an MA degree and in a senior position) for the mighty *Johnston Press*, one of the largest producers of regional newspapers in the UK, currently earns just £10,500 a year – and quotes the starting rate for a trainee graduate as a mere £8,500. From South Wales another despairing staffer suggests there should be a new accolade for the company that wins most awards but still manages to pay its staff the lowest rates. Even quoting a fee per thousand words can be misleading. We all know the effort involved in producing a thousand words may depend on the amount of research required to give them depth and accuracy; it is not just a matter of typing a thousand words and printing them on paper. A free weekly paper often pays a junior reporter as little as £8,000 a year and some recognised (paid-for) weeklies offer little better. At the other end of the scale salaries may rise to as much as £14,000 from local dailies; hardly a fortune in the early 21st century and belying the so-called glamorous high-salaried lifestyle often thought to be enjoyed. Although there is a wide variation in salary scales in various parts of the country and from different newspaper groups, at editor level on a regional daily you could be earning anything from £30,00 upwards per year. As for the nationals, a handful of top editors can more than double that figure as a starting point. And they all started at the bottom, just like you and me.

For the vast majority, journalism is a hard-working, intensely absorbing industry with good financial rewards and a job-satisfaction hard to find elsewhere.

Commissions and money talk

Freelances sometimes mistake exactly what a commission is, thinking they have been offered one when, in truth, they haven't. Such misunderstandings lead to disappointment or resentment for the freelance and, very often, annoyance for the editor concerned. The term covers any type of work, from supplying copy to taking photographs or other work, and it is important to make sure that both parties – you and the editor or commissioning editor – agree on what is being commissioned, whether it is the result of prior negotiation or speculative submission of work.

To avoid errors follow these steps:

- Confirm the name and position on the paper of the person you are dealing with.
- Agree on what the commission covers in wordage, deadline, special points to be covered or made in the copy, etc.
- Agree on the format in which you will deliver the copy – hard copy (sheets of paper), disk, tape or other.
- Unless absolutely impossible, get confirmation of what has been agreed in writing before you start work. If this is not possible, at least write your own statement of what you understand has been agreed and get it to the person commissioning you as soon as you can. A verbal contract is just as binding in law as a written one but you may feel happier to have it in hard copy in your hand.

What to charge and/or offer

It is tempting, as a beginner, to take whatever fee is offered without question and often without even knowing what it's going to be. This laxity will get you little reward, allow the editor to pay you at the lowest rate for the job he thinks he can get away with, keep you there for any future work, undercut other writers for the paper and brand you as totally unprofessional. Worst of all is to agree to be paid only if your copy is published; if you have a commission and complete your part of the deal satisfactorily and on time you must always be paid, whether the copy is eventually published or not. In the unlikely event of it not being published you are entitled to a kill fee which is usually lower than the fee you would have received had the piece seen the light of day, but at least better than nothing at all.

Written contracts are seldom offered to freelances nowadays. They used to be confirmation of intent to serve by one side and security of employment by the other. Clauses dealt with the matter of rights, among other things, agreeing to the normal provisions then obtaining; the writer retained the copyright, licensing it to the paper (a daily) to be released after a period of 14 days. In my case this meant I handed over copyright of everything I wrote for the paper for just a fortnight, after which it reverted to me to use elsewhere and in whatever manner I wished. (I may say that a daily column accumulates an enormous amount of copy over a long period and I have, with the copyright in my sole hands, been able to make extensive and profitable use of it ever since.)

Countless stories are told among working journalists of sharp practice on the part of newspapers and newspaper proprietors in sending out contracts to contributors containing terms and conditions, followed by bold text saying something like '*If you agree to the above offers of engagement you do not need to sign and return this contract. A payment cheque accompanies this contract. Encashment of the cheque will constitute your acceptance of the above offer of engagement on the terms and conditions stated above.*' Such wording is unenforceable in law. The 1882 Bills of Exchange Act specifically bars the use of a cheque for any purpose other than for the payment of money. It cannot be used as part of a contract and certainly not as part of any deal assigning copyright.

So what should you be paid? How can you know what is a fair rate for the job? The National Union of Journalists has an established list of recommended rates but it is important to view them with honest consideration, whether you are a member of the Union or not; some are higher than inexperienced freelances can expect to receive, others are the very minimum for skilled writers with specialised knowledge in their subjects and all are open to negotiation. Remember too that wherever your fees-talk starts, it can come down but is unlikely to go up. When it is being discussed make sure you know when the editor (or his accounts department) intends to pay, whether by cheque or directly into your bank account (of which he will need details) and what expenses he will pay, if any.

NUJ rates of pay

The latest annual NUJ *Freelance Fees Guide* emphasises the great variation in fees offered by newspapers everywhere, particularly deploring the fact that for several years freelance rates paid by provincial papers have not risen in proportion to staff salaries or even by the cost of living. Despite this, making a start on provincial papers continues to offer freelances a sound beginning although initial rates of pay are not exciting. But if/when you find a first-class story, aim high and go straight for the nationals if you want to earn better rates. On the whole tabloids pay more and are easier to negotiate with than broadsheets. The following current figures quoted are basic rates from which negotiations should start:

- Nationals per thousand words: features – £220 to £500 (but depending on the expertise and research required) or more; news – from about £230 but a lot more for exclusivity.
- Regional and provincial papers, particularly the latter, generally pay per line: often only £3 per line for the first ten and 25 to 30 pence per line thereafter.

Pressing for extra money may get you another £20 or so for a tip-off or £50 for a page lead. If you can't imagine using your copy again you may be able to sell it for a one-off fee of perhaps about £50 per 500 words. Rates of pay are usually defined in terms of the number of words written. But view this with caution; the paper could interpret this as payment for words published, which may not be the same thing. And some papers pay varying fees for copy published in different parts of the paper.

Not all papers subscribe to these agreed rates, but the majority do, with the smaller ones usually belonging to parent groups who do. Of course poor-quality work cannot expect to receive much reward, for it is probably not worth a lot – but next time you're offered derisory rates for a first-class job, will you have the courage to ask for a fair rate? The answer to such a request may be a shrug indicating that's what the rate is, take it or leave it. Some journalists say we have to take what is offered or we don't get the work. Not so, say others, perhaps those who can more easily afford to pick and choose. Every time we accept poor pay, they insist, we are hammering another nail in our own coffins. On this matter you must make up your own mind.

Where do you fit in?

'I am not a member of the National Union of Journalists,' you may be saying, 'so do the rates quoted above apply to me, and should I expect to receive them?'

Deciding how much to accept, or to charge if asked to quote a rate for a particular job, is not easy. On the whole it is best to use the NUJ rates as a guide, so at least you know where to start thinking about the rewards for your work. You should also be prepared to be flexible until you're sufficiently well-known for editors to come looking for you (yes, that may take some years) instead of you courting them. At all stages of your writing career you must be ready to negotiate fees – always before writing the relevant copy. You may spend nine or ten hours on one piece and earn £150, or you may toil at research and writing another for five hours and earn £750. Only you can be the judge of where and how to price yourself at the right level for each job without selling yourself short. Believe me, this tricky assessment of what you are worth does become easier with long-term practice and familiarisation with the markets. If you regularly sell to local papers you may begin to perceive a pattern of fees, depending on the nature of the publication and the company producing it. Your normal market study of the readership, the advertising and the paper's general viability will guide you as to whether you are receiving a fair and reasonable return for your work.

There's another most important reason for getting your terms of work straight with every editor you write for. When the time comes to be paid there can be no arguments if everything was firmly agreed in the first place. Most editors are leaned on from above to keep costs down and know that the less it costs to run their papers the greater favour they're likely to find from their owners or proprietors. Naturally they don't want to be expected, let alone forced, to pay more than low rates. It's sad to hear of freelance writers so pleased to have their work accepted that they gratefully accept whatever fee is offered, not even mentioning it until some document reveals how much it's going to be. Can you imagine a worker in any other occupation being content with such a loose and unsatisfactory arrangement? Do you believe the newsprint suppliers, the van drivers, the secretarial staff and all the other people employed in the running of a newspaper don't know their rates of pay? Would management or editors dream of treating them as so many of them treat freelances? Regular staff writers, please note, have a structured and recognised scale of salaries and wouldn't put up with the treatment sometines meted out to freelances. The labour force essential to make a newspaper work depends on writers as much as it does on other employees. Newspapers must, of course, secure the services of staff journalists by paying them a regular and mutually agreed rate and freelances should expect to be treated in the same way. The potential purchaser (the editor) either wants your copy and is prepared to pay for it or doesn't want it and hands it back immediately. Hardened writers may say the newspaper world just doesn't work like this and to some extent I am forced to agree with them – but until we freelances behave like professionals and try to improve the way in which we have traditionally been treated for too long, standards are unlikely to rise.

Getting paid

Most newspapers expect freelances to submit invoices for work done. Large papers in particular have a well-established and practical system of not paying anybody anything unless all the required documentation is in place. Accounts departments who send out payment may not even know fees are due to you if you do not tell them, word not having been passed automatically down the line. The onus is on you to have discovered what the normal procedure is. Some provide claim forms (if asked for them) while others leave it to you to submit your own claims. It is only sensible to find out how it is normally done. Don't give the accounts department an excuse ('We haven't received our official claim form from you') for not paying you on time.

It also makes for reliable book-keeping if you send a claim or an invoice when the work is filed (i.e. delivered by whatever means) or whenever the time for submission is agreed. If you are making your own invoice it should not only indicate how much you should be paid, but when (within 30 days of receipt of invoice is more than generous). Quote your self-employed status and national insurance number on all invoices to demonstrate your professionalism in keeping accurate records. Be aware that if the paper does not expect you to send an invoice you may have to accept whatever arrives if you have not already sorted out the precise figure in advance.

What if they don't pay?

If the paper is late in paying you or fails to pay after a reasonable time, telephone the accounts department with all your details to hand, or write to them or do both. Don't immediately assume they are trying to do you down – although that may be the case – for many instances of late payment are just the result of office inefficiency.

If all else fails warn the paper that you may be obliged to take legal action. This is simple and not wildly expensive, even if the case is lost. County Courts offer a 'small claims' service for the attempted recovery of debts under about £5,000 and it is best to proceed thus:

- Be confident you have a clear solid case without ambiguities or inconsistencies and that the paper you intend to sue has not gone out of business or been absorbed into another company which is not legally obliged to honour your defendant's debts. There is nothing to be gained from flogging a dead horse.
- Over a period of (say) a month, send four weekly invoices by recorded delivery, marking them 'FIRST', 'SECOND' as appropriate, being sure to write this on the invoice as well as on the envelope with each posting. After this time with no satisfaction, send the final invoice stating that unless payment is received within days, that is by (here quote a date), action will be commenced in the County Court to recover the debt.
- If that doesn't work (and it often does) obtain from the Court a copy of the leaflet *How to make a claim*. You will also need a copy of the County Court summons (N1) – in fact it might be a good idea to pick up several so you have some in reserve to strengthen your resolve on future occasions. Most bad payers then pay up. If one defends the case the proceedings will normally be transferred to *his* local court. That could be a long way away so you should ask for travel and out-of-pocket expenses. Normally the settling of the case is itself

informal with you, the defendant or someone speaking on his behalf, any witnesses and the arbitrator together in a small room: no bewigged judges or complex legal formalities. Statements are made by both parties, questions posed and answered, and the decision is made. Often the whole affair lasts less than half an hour.

- Once you have won the case the court will make an order on the defendant to pay within a stated time, usually a fortnight or a month hence. And when you have the settlement cheque in your hands take note of the defendant's account number before paying it into yours. If it bounces you can have his account frozen until it clears. Justice isn't all on the side of the baddies. One other small point: should you *lose* or fail to receive the money even after winning, put it down to experience. And recoup any losses by writing about it for the benefit of others who may one day find themselves in a similar situation (which is what I am doing here).

Useful contacts

- *Headlines*, The Newspaper Society, 74 Great Russell Street, London WC1B 3DA *tel* 020 7636 7014 *email* ns@newspapersoc.org.uk *website* www.newspapersoc.org.uk (bi-monthly magazine dedicated to providing news and information about the regional and local newspaper industry)
- *National Council for the Training of Journalists*, Latton Bush Centre, Southern Way, Harlow, Essex CM18 7BL *tel* 01279 430009 *email* info@nctj.com *website* www.nctj.com
- *Careers in Journalism*, National Union of Journalists, 308 Gray's Inn Road, London WC1X 8DP *tel* 020 7278 7916 *email* acorn.house@nuj.org.uk *website* http://www.nuj.org.uk
- *Chartered Institute of Taxation*, 12 Upper Belgrave Street, London SW1X 8BB *tel* 020 7235 9381 *email* post@tax.org.uk *website* www.tax.org.uk
- Association of Tax Technicians, 12 Upper Belgrave Street, London SW1X 8BB *tel* 020 7235 2544
- *Data Protection Act 1998*, Her Majesty's Stationery Office, St Clements House, 2–16 Colegate, Norwich NR3 1BQ *tel* 01603 723011

- *Official Secrets Act 1989*, Her Majesty's Stationery Office, St Clements House, 2–16 Colegate, Norwich NR3 1BQ *tel* 01603 723011
- *The Press Complaints Commission**, 1 Salisbury Square, London EC4Y 8JB *tel* 020 7353 3732 *email* pcc@pcc.org.uk *website* www.pcc.org.uk
- *Advertising Standards Authority*, 2 Torrington Place, London WC1E 7HW *tel* 020 7580 5555 *email* inquiries@asa.org.uk *website* www.asa.org.uk
- *International Federation of Journalists*, Residence Palace, 155 rue de la Loi, 1040 Brussels, Belgium *email* ifj@ifj.org *website* www.ifj.org (the world's largest organisation of journalists representing around 450,000 members in more than 100 countries)
- *FAIR*, 112 W. 27th Street, New York, NY 10001 *tel* 212-633-6700 *email* fair@fair.org *website* www.fair.org (the national media watch group)
- *Committee to Protect Journalists*, 330 Seventh Avenue, 12th Floor, New York NY 10001 *website* www.cpj.org
- *Index on Censorship website* www.indexonline.org (founded in 1972 by Stephen Spender to protect the basic human right of free expression)

*The Press Complaints Commission (PCC) is charged with enforcing the following Code of Practice which was framed by the newspaper and periodical industry and ratified in December 1999.

All members of the press have a duty to maintain the highest professional and ethical standards. This Code sets the benchmark for those standards. It both protects the rights of the individual and upholds the public's right to know. The Code is the cornerstone of the system of self-regulation to which the industry has made a binding commitment. Editors and publishers must ensure that the Code is observed rigorously not only by their staff but also by anyone who contributes to their publications. It is essential to the workings of an agreed code that it be honoured not only to the letter but in the full spirit. The Code should not be interpreted so narrowly as to compromise its commitment to respect the rights of the individual, nor so broadly that it prevents publication in the public interest. It is the responsibility of editors to co-operate with the PCC as swiftly as possible in the resolution of complaints. Any publication which is criticised by the PCC under one of the following clauses must print the adjudication which follows in full and with due prominence.

1 *Accuracy*

i) Newspapers and periodicals should take care not to publish inaccurate, misleading or distorted material including pictures.

ii) Whenever it is recognised that a significant inaccuracy, misleading statement or distorted report has been published, it should be corrected promptly and with due prominence.

iii) An apology must be published whenever appropriate.

iv) Newspapers, whilst free to be partisan, must distinguish clearly between comment, conjecture and fact.

v) A newspaper or periodical must report fairly and accurately the outcome of an action for defamation to which it has been a party.

2 *Opportunity to reply*

A fair opportunity for reply to inaccuracies must be given to individuals or organisations when reasonably called for.

3 *Privacy*

i) Everyone is entitled to respect for his or her private and family life, home, health and correspondence. A publication will be expected to justify intrusions into any individual's private life without consent.

ii) The use of long lens photography to take pictures of people in private places without their consent is unacceptable. Note – Private places are public or private property where there is a reasonable expectation of privacy.

4 *Harassment*

i) Journalists and photographers must neither obtain nor seek to obtain information or pictures through intimidation, harassment or persistent pursuit.

ii) They must not photograph individuals in private places (as defined by the note to clause 3) without their consent; must not persist in telephoning, questioning, pursuing or photographing individuals after having been asked to desist; must not remain on their property after having been asked to leave and must not follow them.

iii) Editors must ensure that those working for them comply with these requirements and must not publish material from other sources which does not meet these requirements.

5 *Intrusion into grief or shock*

In cases involving personal grief or shock, enquiries should be carried out and approaches made with sympathy and discretion. Publication must be handled sensitively at such times but this should not be interpreted as restricting the right to report judicial proceedings.

6 *Children*

i) Young people should be free to complete their time at school without unnecessary intrusion.

ii) Journalists must not interview or photograph a child under the age of

16 on subjects involving the welfare of the child or any other child in the absence of or without the consent of a parent or other adult who is responsible for the children.

iii) Pupils must not be approached or photographed while at school without the permission of the school authorities.

iv) There must be no payment to minors for material involving the welfare of children nor payments to parents or guardians for material about their children or wards unless it is demonstrably in the child's interest.

v) Where material about the private life of a child is published, there must be justification for publication other than the fame, notoriety or position of his or her parents or guardian.

7 *Children in sex cases*

1 *The press must not, even where the law does not prohibit it, identify children under the age of 16 who are involved in cases concerning sexual offences, whether as victims or as witnesses.*

2 *In any press report of a case involving a sexual offence against a child –*

i) The child must not be identified.

ii) The adult may be identified.

iii) The word 'incest' must not be used where a child victim might be identified.

iv) Care must be taken that nothing in the report implies the relationship between the accused and the child.

8 *Listening devices*

Journalists must not obtain or publish material obtained by using clandestine listening devices or by intercepting private telephone conversations.

9 *Hospitals*

i) Journalists or photographers making enquiries at hospitals or similar institutions should identify themselves to a responsible executive and obtain permission before entering non-public areas.

ii) The restrictions on intruding into privacy are particularly relevant to enquiries about individuals in hospitals or similar institutions.

10 *Reporting of crime*

i) The press must avoid identifying relatives or friends of persons convicted or accused of crime without their consent.

ii) Particular regard should be paid to the potentially vulnerable position of children who are witnesses to, or victims of, crime. This should not be interpreted as restricting the right to report judicial proceedings.

11 *Misrepresentation*

i) Journalists must not generally obtain or seek to obtain information or pictures through misrepresentation or subterfuge.

ii) Documents or photographs should be removed only with the consent of the owner.

iii) Subterfuge can be justified only in the public interest and only when material cannot be obtained by any other means.

12 *Victims of sexual assault*

The press must not identify victims of sexual assault or publish material likely to contribute to such identification unless there is adequate justification and, by law, they are free to do so.

13 *Discrimination*

i) The press must avoid prejudicial or pejorative reference to a person's race, colour, religion, sex or sexual orientation or to any physical or mental illness or disability.

ii) It must avoid publishing details of a person's race, colour, religion, sexual orientation, physical or mental illness or disability unless these are directly relevant to the story.

14 *Financial journalism*

i) Even where the law does not prohibit it, journalists must not use for their own profit financial information they receive in advance of its general publication, nor should they pass such information to others.

ii) They must not write about shares or securities in whose performance they know that they or their close families have a significant financial interest without disclosing the interest to the editor or financial editor.

iii) They must not buy or sell, either directly or through nominees or agents, shares or securities about which they have written recently or about which they intend to write in the near future.

15 *Confidential sources*

Journalists have a moral obligation to protect confidential sources of information.

16 *Payment for articles*

i) Payment or offers of payment for stories or information must not be made directly or through agents to witnesses or potential witnesses in current criminal proceedings except where the material concerned ought to be published in the public interest and there is an overriding need to make or promise to make a payment for this to be done. Journalists must take every possible step to ensure that no financial dealings have influence on the evidence that those witnesses may give. (An editor authorising such a payment must be prepared to demonstrate that there is a legitimate public interest at stake involving matters that the public has a right to know. The payment or, where accepted, the offer of payment to any witness who is actually cited to give evidence should be disclosed to the prosecution and the defence and the witness should be advised of this).

ii) Payment or offers of payment for stories, pictures or information, must not be made directly or through agents to convicted or confessed criminals or to their associates – who may include family, friends and colleagues – except where the material concerned ought to be published in the public interest and payment is necessary for this to be done.
The public interest includes:
i) Detecting or exposing crime or a serious misdemeanour.
ii) Protecting public health and safety.
iii) Preventing the public from being misled by some statement or action of an individual or organisation.
In any case where the public interest is invoked, the Press Complaints Commission will require a full explanation by the editor demonstrating how the public interest was served.
There is a public interest in freedom of expression itself. The Commission will therefore have regard to the extent to which material has, or is about to, become available to the public. In cases involving children editors must demonstrate an exceptional public interest to over-ride the normally paramount interest of the child.

Running the Press Complaints Commission, so frequently criticised for having no real teeth, is evidently well worthwhile. When forced to stand down from his job as part-time chairman early in 2002 over his involvement in the collapse of the American energy giant *Enron*, former Cabinet Minister Lord Wakeham was £156,000 a year poorer.

More contacts

- School of Journalism, Media and Cultural Studies, University of Wales College of Cardiff *website* www.cf.ac.uk/jomec
- University of Central Lancashire, Department of Journalism, Preston PR1 2HE *tel* 01772 894730 *email* webmaster@uk journalism.org *website* www.uclan.ac.uk/facs/lbs/depts/ journ (Postgraduate Diploma in Newspaper Journalism, MA/PGdip Online Journalism, BA (Hons) Journalism, and a BA(Hons) Journalism and English)
- Department of Journalism, City University, Northampton Square, London EC1V 0HB *tel* 020 7040 8221 *email* journalism@city.ac.uk *website* www.city.ac.uk/journalism
- Communication Skills Europe *website* www.cseltd.com (editorial and publishing management courses for journalists, editors and publishing managers)

- Cornwall College *website* www.cornwall.ac.uk (18-week postgraduate courses, starting September and February: two-year Higher National Diploma in Newspaper and Magazine Journalism)
- Darlington College of Technology, School of Journalism *website* www.darlington.ac.uk (NCTJ accredited, NCTJ pre-entry courses, BTEC Media Studies National Diploma and Britain's only International Diploma in Journalism: open to non-UK students)
- Edge Hill College of Higher Education, Ormskirk, Lancashire *website* www.edgehill.ac.uk (BA (Hons) Journalism degree course accredited by Lancaster University & NCTJ – also offer degree courses in New Media and Media & Communication)
- European Journalism Centre *website* www.ejc.nl (independent, non-profit institute for further training, a forum for journalists, media executives and journalism educators)
- Glasgow Caledonian University, City Campus, 70 Cowcaddens Road, Glasgow G4 0BA *tel* 0141 331 3000
- Journalism Training Centre, Unit G Mill Green Road, Mitcham, Surrey CR4 4HT *tel* 020-8640 3696 *website* www.journalism-training-centre.co.uk (14-week vocational training courses, starting January, May and September each year)
- London Institute, London College of Printing *website* www.linst.ac.uk/lcp/courses/media.html (offers a range of courses including a BA in Journalism)
- London School of Journalism, 22 Upbrook Mews, Bayswater, London W2 3HG *tel* 0207 706 3790 *email* redweb@lsjinfo.net *website* www.lsj.org
- Media and Communication Studies at the University of Wales, Aberystwyth *website* www.aber.ac.uk/media/Functions/mcs.html (first-class site, including an enormous resource of media and communications links)
- The Periodicals Training Council *website* www.ppa.co.uk/ptc
- Hold the Front Page website www.holdthefront page.co.uk (named the Best Overall Journalism Service in the 2002 European Online Journalism Awards)
- University of Sheffield, Department of Journalism Studies *website* www.shef.ac.uk/~j (MA in Journalism Studies)

- The Thomson Foundation *website* www.thomsonfoundation.co.uk (the oldest international media training organisation in the world)
- AlphaGalileo *website* www.alphagalileo.org (news centre for European science, medicine and technology)
- Euronews *website* www.euronews.net (news provided by a consortium of 18 European public broadcasters)
- ForeignWire *website* www.foreignwire.com (review of international affairs from ex-*Independent* and *Newsweek* reporters)
- Future Events News Service *website* www.fens.com (forthcoming news events)
- Public Records Office *website* www.pro.gov.uk

'*Imagination is more important than knowledge.*' Albert Einstein

11. Over to You

Every published writer began as a raw beginner but real writers have learned to keep professionalism, persistence and productivity firmly in mind. These are the keys to satisfaction for yourself and cash for your pocket. Professionalism in all you write, everyone you contact and all your dealings. Persistence in not giving up. Never take 'no' for a final answer: it may just be nudging you to a different approach and stretching your writing horizons. Productivity in having plenty of copy on the go at the same time. Writer's block doesn't exist.

Journalists do not enjoy a good press. 'It's appalling,' is the comment when the truth about a story comes to light and proves the paper's version of what happened was highly dramatised just to make a good story. So given you had the task of maintaining and increasing circulation and you were sitting in the editor's chair, how would you behave? You'd have the advertisers to think about too, for they are the ones who pay most of the bills, as this book has shown. Of course none of that excuses lies or dishonesty. You don't have to print what is not true or in any way compromise the integrity of your staff or yourself. But what about that oft-repeated phrase 'freedom of the press'?

How would we expose child cruelty, for instance, and the evils of pornography, if we did not support a press free to inform us about it? And what about bringing corrupt politicians and businessmen (among many others) to justice? If we are not kept informed by an investigative and watchful press, criminals and fraudsters of all kinds, dishonest practices and the wickedness of apparently quite ordinary people may be allowed to flourish unchecked. Next time you hear anyone criticising the press for intruding into people's private lives or harassing people for a story, remember all is not always what it seems to be.

There are many questions to ask ourselves about the morals of what we write. Is it right to employ subterfuge to get the facts on the story you know your readers will want to read? Are hidden tape recorders and cameras justifiable? Or not telling someone when you are recording his words? Many questions – and the answers do not come easily.

The retouching of pictures is commonplace and there is no doubt that it greatly improves quality. But retouching with intent to deceive? The NUJ has taken steps to see that doctored pix are always identified as such. In 1995 photographer Crispin Rodwell took legal action over his shot of a boy throwing a ball at a wall bearing the graffiti *Time for Peace*. This slogan was changed to *Recipes for Peace* for a cover for a cookery book to be sold in aid of a children`s charity. Then it was doctored again for a *Sky TV* advertising hoarding. Graphic plagiarism or justifiable re-use of a good picture?

'It's in the interest of the public,' is the defence of newspaper editors when under fire from outraged critics. But is it always? In March 2002 Lord Chief Justice Lord Woolf ruled that a ban on naming a married Premier League footballer who had affairs with two women would be an unjustified interference with the freedom of the press. '*If newspapers do not publish information which the public is interested in, there will be fewer newspapers published*,' he said, '*which will not be in the public interest.*'

In general it is accepted that although everyone is entitled to a private life, public figures are of great interest to readers and it is hardly reasonable for those who court public attention to complain when they find rather more is revealed about their private lives than they might like.

Chequebook journalism

The practice of newspapers paying witnesses in criminal trials is another area of controversy but one which may soon be resolved by law. Until now one lobby has claimed that banning such payment would be a restriction on freedom of speech and that payments are justified because papers couldn't get the stories without paying important witnesses. Opponents argue that paying witnesses is for commercial gain to get 'exclusivity' and increase sales, which itself denies rival papers freedom of speech. So is such 'chequebook journalism' a charter for freedom?

So wild are the sums being paid to key witnesses in banner-headline trials that early in 2000 the government began considering plans to make payments to witnesses criminal acts in themselves. From the cash deal promised to a prosecution witness by the *News of the World* in the 1966 trial of Moors murderers Ian Brady and Myra Hindley, to the £25,000 the *Sunday Telegraph* offered to prosecution witness Peter Bessell in the 1979 Jeremy Thorpe trial, and the dozen or more witnesses who were paid up to £30,000 each at the trial of Rosemary West in 1995 – dangling large sums of money in front of witnesses may have disturbing effects. Is evidence likely to be exaggerated by the prospect of a large cheque? Does the temptation to 'say the right thing' in order to qualify for the pay-out distort the course of justice? Do witnesses withhold evidence so as to grant to a paper that's paying them exclusive coverage when the trial is over? Should people with a good story to tell be paid, or should sources never be rewarded? When two British nurses, found guilty of murder, were released from a Saudi Arabian jail in 1998 both were paid highly, one by the *Daily Express* and the other by the *Mirror* – all, according to the Press Complaints Commission, 'in the public interest'. We must also remember the position of the press itself.

Reporters, particularly young inexperienced journalists perhaps on their first big story or desperate for a real scoop to boost their promotion prospects, can sometimes be bought. 'Freebies' may be pressed on writers who can put the donor in a good light – and it is not always easy to refuse. And what about being bribed *not* to report what your instincts tell you would be of interest ot readers? 'Buying' works both ways; money talks. Teacher Amy Gehring's acquittal in 2000 of having sex with under-age boys led to them being offered sums up to £10,000 each by leading tabloids. At last it seems that the press itself is thinking enough is enough – or it is finding it too expensive to continue paying witnesses for their stories? If new government thinking becomes law, it will be an offence to make payments, or make arrangements to do so, until such trials are finished.

In a bizarre twist to the meaning of 'chequebook journalism', the organisers (a militant Islamic group) of a press conference at a central London hotel in August 2002 tried to charge journalists a £30 admission fee. This unprecedented step left the conference more than half empty. A spokesman for the organisers defended the decision to charge for access. 'The press are normally more than willing to pay for stories, so I don't think this is any different,' he said. 'We have got Muslim leaders from all over the country together for you, so we think it's reasonable to ask you to pay for the privilege of hearing them speak.' After heated scenes, journalists were asked to leave.

Power: use or abuse?

What are the ethical matters to consider? *Guardian* editor Peter Preston, keen to expose Tory politicians accepting cash payment in return for asking loaded question in the House, was himself accused of overstepping the mark (in the use of what was said to be a less-than-honest fax) in an attempt to get the story he wanted. In a similar situation member of Parliament Jonathan Aitken (an ex-journalist and great-nephew of *Daily Express* owner Lord Beaverbrook) was proved to have been lying about a bill paid to the Ritz hotel during a libel case against the *Guardian*, and went to prison.

Celebrities and 'top' people often complain they have been treated badly by the press. Let there be the slightest suspicion of misbehaviour, especially of a personal, marital or sexual nature, and the tabloids are on the spot. There's a cynical old rhyme:

Dish the dirt, spill the beans,
Tell us about behind the scenes.
Spill the beans, dish the dirt,
Do not worry who you hurt.

Is this hounding famous people who have a right to privacy in their personal lives, or are reporters doing a public service in bringing down the mighty in their misdemeanours? Whatever you think, if reporters did *not* report such matters we should not be in a position to make our own judgement about whether it is right or wrong. And banning reporting could be called censorship or hiding the truth . . . Perhaps the press can't win, however it behaves.

Many local newspapers would be very thin if men stopped getting drunk, fighting each other, committing petty theft and beating their partners. When we complain about the contents of newspapers, we must remember that they would stop featuring spicy stories if the public didn't want to read them, just as your local cut-price shop would go out of business if nobody bought its goods.

The introduction of radio and television threatened papers in the past. In just four years the internet has reached seven-eighths of our population. 'The end of the printed newspaper!' cry the doomsters. Will newspapers live on and continue to flourish, despite the wavering fortunes of some, in these rapidly changing times? Yet another red-top was launched from the Express stable late in 2002: the confusingly titled *Daily Star Sunday*. With the long-standing bitter rivalry between tabloid competitors reaching new heights (depths?) will it survive?

We've come a long way since the art of printing from a single wooden block was known in the 6th century AD in China and the first movable type was used there in the 11th century. In Europe we had to wait until the 15th century for it to be reinvented (traditionally by Johannes Gutenberg in Germany) before William Caxton introduced it in England. Big names of the past, like Beaverbrook, Northcliffe and Rothermere, are not necessarily signposts to the future. Optimism and enthusiasm certainly are.

Newspapers not just ink on paper; they are alive and fast-moving. Insatiable, they eat *today* and are hungry for *tomorrow*.

Will you help feed them? They're waiting . . .

Index